NICK STELLINO'S

Passione

PASTA, PIZZA, and PANINI

*Food photography
by E. J. Armstrong*

G. P. PUTNAM'S SONS
NEW YORK

The recipes in this book are to be followed exactly as written.
Neither the publisher nor the author is responsible for your specific health or allergy needs
that may require medical supervision, or for any adverse reactions to the recipes in this book.

G. P. Putnam's Sons
Publishers Since 1838
a member of Penguin Putnam Inc.
375 Hudson Street
New York, NY 10014

Black-and-white photographs by Nanci Stellino

Library of Congress Cataloging-in-Publication Data

Stellino, Nick.
[Passione]
Nick Stellino's Passione : pasta, pizza, and panini / Nick Stellino.
p.   cm.
ISBN 0-399-14657-1
1. Cookery (Pasta).   2. Pizza.   3. Sandwiches.   4. Cookery, Italian.   I. Title.
TX809.M17 S723   2000   00-040269
641.5945—dc21

Printed in the United States of America
1   3   5   7   9   10   8   6   4   2

This book is printed on acid-free paper. ∞

BOOK DESIGN BY DEBORAH KERNER

BOLLA.
BOLLA WINES OF ITALY

Proud sponsors of *Nick Stellino's Family Kitchen* on public television.

TO MY FATHER, VINCENZO,
WHO TAUGHT ME HOW TO DREAM,
AND TO MY MOTHER,
MASSIMILIANA,
WHO TAUGHT ME HOW TO LOVE.

Acknowledgments

This book is the result of great cooperation among many people. I would like to thank Phyllis Grann and John Duff at Putnam for believing in my work. As usual, E. J. Armstrong did magic with her photographs, which were beautifully styled by Patty Wittman. Once again Susan Volland and Deb Winson accepted my invitation to collaborate with me in testing the recipes. I also thank my co-dreamers Jeff Gentes and Jay Parikh, who, together with Andrew Mansinne and Mike Wolf, helped me turn this book into a television series for public television.

Thanks to my family for believing in my dreams: my mother and father, Massimiliana and Vincenzo; my brother, Mario; my aunt Buliti and uncle Michele, cousins Gerri and Veronica, aunt Titi and uncle Franz, cousins Attila and Tiziana; my in-laws Sol, Gitte, Toby, and Alan; and my nephews Josh and Andrew.

None of this would have happened without my wife, Nanci, the center of my universe. In a world that keeps changing, she is my one true thing.

Contents

Introduction   1

Pasta   7

Gnocchi   91

Risotto   105

Pizza   125

Panini   173

Basics   219

Index   257

Introduction

❦ou might wonder why I've chosen *Passione* as the title for this cookbook. In my case, it's entirely appropriate, because it is indeed passion that drove me to embark on a culinary career. I remember falling in love with food early in my childhood at my grandmother's knee. She showed me there was art even in sautéing garlic, and to this day, it's one of the things I do best. The kitchen in my parents' house was where the family gathered, and some of our most memorable moments took place there. So to me, food means more than just fuel for the body; it also means warmth, love, happiness, and good cheer.

When I cook, I manage to forget all the terrible things that might have happened throughout the day. As I stand before the stove, listening to the olive oil sizzle, I enter the world of my passion. This book is about sharing that passion with you, in hope that you too will fall in love as much with the preparation of food as with eating it.

As you look at these recipes, keep in mind that this is a book about enjoying yourself, having fun while you pursue a passion. Yes, cooking ought to be fun. Too many people approach it as if they were engaging in battle, or planning a major negotiation, or competing in a contest. Well, cooking is none of those things. If you do not cook with a smile in your heart, your food will not taste good.

Just as important as the act of cooking, then, is the attitude you bring to it. Approach it with a sense of adventure, with a lightness of spirit, and even your "mistakes" will be delicious. I realize some of my greatest passion in cooking, but believe me, I've burned plenty of food in my time. And I still make plenty of mistakes. While in life there are mistakes we can never rectify, things we can never take back, in the kitchen we can always start again.

After all, what is failure? As far as I'm concerned, it is simply a stepping stone on the path to glory. Every time you make a mistake in the kitchen, you are that much closer to getting it right the next time. If only from a statistical point of view, making mistakes is a good thing. If you make a mistake and understand what you've done wrong, then and there you have learned something. It's also possible that by making a mistake, unwittingly, unexpectedly, you discover a great new recipe. As I tell the students in my cooking classes and anyone who cooks with me at home, making a mistake in the kitchen is just part of the process of learning the art and craft of cooking.

THE RULES

In cooking, as in all endeavors, there are rules. The two that I set forth for your culinary education are simple:

Rule 1. There are no rules.
Rule 2. Rules are made to be broken.

Though I've numbered them, I couldn't decide which really should take first or second place. I'll leave that for you to decide.

Yet if there are no rules, and if they're made to be broken, why do I give such specific, detailed instructions on how to re-create the dishes in this book? Very simply because the recipes represent my interpretation of these dishes. Most have been prepared by millions of Italians, from home cooks to professional chefs, who each interpret them in their own particular way. The cooking traditions themselves are centuries old, and rooted in the regions of Italy that nurtured them; the variations are as many as the cooks who have ever prepared the dishes.

When I was growing up, the usual limits of my universe were three or four square blocks of my neighborhood. Everybody there knew one another, if only by name, and all us kids knew one another. As often as not, we would be in one another's homes at lunchtime, snacktime, dinnertime. Even as children, we knew

Passione

that one mother's interpretation of tomato sauce, pizza, roast, or pasta would differ from another's. Sure, the basic ingredients would be the same—after all, we were all Italians—but each household brought its own character to meals.

The point I'm trying to make is that no one, including me, holds the copyright on what is "authentic Italian." In fact, authentic cuisine from any culture is constantly evolving, from cook to cook, family to family, generation to generation. And even though a recipe is based on certain standard combinations of ingredients and techniques, it is the personal interpretation of each chef that makes it unique and keeps culinary traditions alive.

Even if there are no rules, and the meaning of "authentic" may change from time to time, we should still be aware of what is right and what is wrong. When food tastes good, that is right. When it doesn't, that is wrong.

And just who makes these decisions about what tastes good or not? In my own kitchen, when I cook, I figure I'm the boss. I make the decisions, although my wife may offer the occasional well-intentioned and welcome suggestion. In your kitchen, when you cook—even if you're cooking the recipes in this book— you're the boss. Keep this in mind and understand that you should never let the fear of failure stop you from trying something new.

Nothing in this book is intended to enslave you to a set of rules. But if you learn the basics, for instance how to cook pasta in a way that will enhance its qualities, or how to mix ingredients to get the best consistency for gnocchi, you will be free to follow your own creative spirit, and to contribute to your own culinary traditions.

THE THREE PASSIONS

This book is about the kind of food that I love most, and in this collection of recipes I have, accordingly, indulged my passions. First pasta: From lasagna and tortellini to pasta medallions and ravioli, I have included dishes drawn from the classic—or, if you will, "authentic"—versions in my homeland and from innovations inspired by my travels throughout the Mediterranean and the States. And then there are the worthy "cousins" of pasta, gnocchi and risotto, which recently have been enjoying a glorious reception on the tables of diners around the world.

Indeed, gnocchi is one of my favorite dishes, and bringing its special appeal to you is a goal of this book.

Pizza perhaps is among the most common prepared foods—in fact, it's hard to find a city or town without a number of places where you can stop for a slice or two, or phone in an order. For me, pizza is the food of my childhood. But pizza is not simply an everyday food for children or a last resort for take-out. There are so many variations that you can enjoy it for a quick snack or a full, elegant meal. Most Americans know the thin- and thick-crust varieties; here I offer another choice, for which I have a special affection: stuffed pizza, a wonderful Italian rendition that differs from region to region. Each version is full of interesting ingredients and very simple to assemble.

And finally, sandwiches, or what we Italians call *panini*. In this book I present interpretations of panini that you might find in Italian shops and restaurants, as well as some recipes of my own invention. They are all easy to make, so you can serve them as a snack, yet distinctive and tasty enough to be a main dish at lunch or supper.

Exploring the traditions of my native country and refining these recipes has been an inspiring enterprise. I hope this book will bring you the same sense of discovery and joy that I have felt.

From my heart to your kitchen,

Nick Stellino

Pasta

I love pasta. If I could, I would eat it every day. As a matter of fact, growing up in Sicily, I did. It's no surprise, then, that this is my favorite section of the book.

Pasta is the number-one Italian dish, popular in Italy and around the world, because it is inexpensive, easy to prepare, and most important, versatile. There's almost nothing you can't do with pasta as a starting point. Whether dry or fresh; whether stuffed, boiled, or baked; whether accompanied by a classic tomato sauce or an innovative combination of vegetables, meat, or fish, pasta can be prepared in an infinity of ways—all of them enticing.

There are many questions and old cooks' tales about preparing pasta, and this seems the time and place for me to offer some thoughts on a few of them.

To salt or not to salt: It's really a matter of personal taste. I prefer a dash of salt added to the boiling water before I put the pasta in to cook. Without salt, the flavor of the pasta will differ slightly, but with a full-flavored sauce you will hardly notice the lack of salt.

Oil in the cooking water: Many people believe that adding oil will prevent the pasta from sticking together. All it will do, I think, is add a bit of flavor. If the pasta is cooked properly, that is, for the right amount of time in enough water to let it move about easily, it shouldn't stick together in the cooking pot. Once you drain the pasta, however, you must cover it with the sauce immediately, or toss it with olive oil if you are not going to sauce it at once. If you leave drained pasta standing, even for only a few minutes, it will clump together, forming what we Italians lovingly call a *mattone di pasta,* or "pasta brick."

Cooking times: Most packages of dry pasta recommend cooking times, varying according to the pasta size, thickness, and so on. I like my pasta cooked just barely tender to the bite, or al dente. To cook dry or fresh pasta, always start out with fresh, cold water, and bring it to a rolling boil. I recommend cooking the pasta for about 8 to 10 minutes, more or less, depending on the type of pasta. Angel-hair pasta, for example, cooks in just a few minutes.

Saucing the pasta: In all my recipes, I instruct you to make the sauce first and keep it at a simmer while you prepare the pasta. Then, in many recipes, I tell you to toss the pasta into the sauce instead of ladling the pasta into a big dish or individual serving dishes and pouring the sauce on top. When you toss the pasta into the sauce, you allow the sauce to penetrate the inner core of the pasta itself, so that sauce and pasta become one. If you prefer lots of sauce (and individual distribution), you can always serve extra on the side.

Tossing the pasta: On my TV show and in cooking demonstrations, I often toss the pasta with the sauce in a large sauté pan, flipping it up in the air, almost like a juggler. But this little trick occasionally backfires, leaving bits of noodle and sauce on the counter and the floor. On television, of course, the incriminating film ends up on the floor of the editing room. To avoid a mess, put the drained pasta back into the cooking pot and return the pot to the stovetop. Add the sauce and, over medium-low heat, toss the pasta and sauce safely in the pot for 2 to 3 minutes. Then you're ready to serve.

All the sauces in this book are simple to make, and suitable for almost any type of pasta, fresh or dry. You can experiment with a wide range of shapes and sizes. Try a different brand of pasta from your usual choice. Try various shapes with your favorite sauce. Kids love the crinkled radiatore pasta and bite-size ziti, which are easier and less messy to eat than long strands of spaghetti or linguine. (Some adults who are not too adept at twirling pasta around a fork might agree.) Or try a new sauce, from one of the many possibilities in this book, on your family's favorite pasta.

Most important, have fun and eat well.

Dry Pasta

*D*ry pasta comes in many shapes and forms: linguine, penne, penne rigate, rigatoni, spaghetti, tortiglioni, and so on. To the uninitiated, matters could become confusing. Which pasta is the right one to use? In the recipes I give recommendations about which cut of pasta I believe will work best. Yet you should not be limited by my suggestions; use whatever pasta you like and are confident with. I do, however, encourage you to experiment.

Since "fresh" pasta has become so much more readily available in America, some people have, misguidedly, relegated dry pasta to second place. But frequently, for certain recipes, a good dry pasta is the right choice. More often than not, dry pasta will hold up better with a robust sauce. For many people, dry pasta is simply more convenient. And you don't have to sacrifice taste for convenience; there are many good dry pastas, domestic and imported. I have to confess a prejudice for dry pasta made in Italy. Italian-made pastas seem to hold together better during cooking, while pastas produced elsewhere tend to soften too quickly and miss that perfect al dente texture.

Baked Pasta with Eggplant Sauce

PASTA AL FORNO CON SUGO DI MELANZANE

Sicilian eggplant is a delicacy, and combined with sausage, it reaches celestial heights of flavor. This baked dish, one of my childhood favorites, surely will become a favorite of yours.

SERVES 6

6 tablespoons olive oil, plus additional for greasing

½ cup Italian-Style Bread Crumbs (page 220)

6 large cloves garlic, thickly sliced

½ teaspoon red pepper flakes

1 medium eggplant (1 pound), cut into ½-inch cubes

1 pound Italian-style sausage, casing removed, cut into ½-inch pieces

½ cup red wine

1½ cups Tomato Sauce (page 229)

1 cup Beef Stock (page 221)

½ teaspoon salt

¼ teaspoon freshly ground black pepper

1 pound ziti, penne, or small shells

8 ounces fresh or smoked mozzarella or scamorza, cut into ¼-inch dice (see Chef's Tips)

½ cup freshly grated Romano cheese

Preheat the oven to 425°. Bring a large pot of salted water to a boil. Brush or spray a 9x13-inch lasagna pan or baking dish with olive oil, and coat with half the bread crumbs.

Heat the 6 tablespoons oil over medium-high heat in a large sauté pan or skillet, add the garlic and red pepper flakes, and cook until the garlic is lightly browned, about 1 minute. In two batches, fry the eggplant in the oil until it is brown on all sides, about 4 minutes. Remove the eggplant and garlic to a plate or bowl, and keep warm. In the same pan or skillet, brown the sausage. Pour in the wine, stirring to dislodge any browned bits from the bottom of the pan, and then simmer to reduce the liquid by half, about 2 minutes. Return the eggplant to the pan and add the Tomato Sauce, stock, salt, and pepper. Bring the mixture to a boil, reduce the

continued

heat, and simmer, stirring occasionally, until you have a nice, rich sauce, about 15 minutes.

While the sauce simmers, cook the pasta in the boiling water according to package directions (see Chef's Tips). Drain, and return the pasta to the empty pot. Pour the sauce over the pasta, and toss the two together, along with the mozzarella or scamorza and half the Romano. Spoon mixture into the prepared lasagna pan, and sprinkle with the remaining Romano and bread crumbs. Bake until a brown crust forms on top, about 20 minutes. Serve hot.

Chef's Tips: *If using fresh mozzarella that was packed in water, drain well on paper towels before dicing.*

It's better to undercook the pasta on the stovetop, as it will continue to cook in the oven.

$\mathcal{B}$aked Pasta with Sausage and Zucchini

PASTA AL FORNO CON SALSICCIA E ZUCCHINE

Zucchini are an underappreciated vegetable, and few people know how to extract their real flavor. Try this recipe and you will never feel the same about zucchini again.

SERVES 6

1 tablespoon unsalted butter

½ cup Italian-Style Bread Crumbs (page 220)

1 pound small zucchini, quartered lengthwise and cut into ½-inch pieces

1 teaspoon salt

½ medium sweet onion

½ large stalk celery, or 1 small stalk from the heart

½ large or 1 small carrot

3 ounces pancetta, cut into chunks, or bacon, cut into pieces

4 to 6 tablespoons olive oil

6 cloves garlic, thickly sliced

¾ pound spicy Italian-style sausage, casing removed, broken up

¾ cup red wine

1¾ cups Tomato Sauce (page 229)

1¾ cups Beef Stock (page 221)

1 pound rigatoni or ziti

4 ounces smoked mozzarella, grated

¼ cup freshly grated Romano cheese

Preheat the oven to 350°. Bring a large pot of salted water to a boil. Generously butter a 9x12-inch casserole pan, and coat with half the bread crumbs.

Place the zucchini in a colander and sprinkle with the salt. Cover with a plate (press down on the zucchini), weighted down with a heavy object. The salt will draw the liquid from the zucchini; the plate will help squeeze it out. Allow the zucchini to sit for about 20 minutes.

Put the onion, celery, carrot, and pancetta or bacon in the bowl of a food processor, and pulse until the mixture is chopped into tiny pieces.

In a large, deep sauté pan, heat 2 tablespoons of the oil over medium-high heat. Add the vegetable-pancetta mixture and the garlic, and sauté for 5 to 6 minutes. Add the sausage, stirring to break it up further, and cook for 4 to 6 minutes, until

continued

the sausage is cooked through. Add the wine, scraping up any browned bits from the bottom of the pan, and cook for 1 to 2 minutes. Add the Tomato Sauce and stock.

Bring the sauce to a boil, reduce the heat, and simmer for 10 to 15 minutes. You should have a thin rather than thick pasta sauce; you want it liquid, as the mixture will eventually bake. Set the sauce aside, and cook the pasta in the boiling water according to the package directions. Do not overcook; the pasta should hold its shape.

While the pasta is cooking, rinse the zucchini. Wrap in a clean, dry kitchen towel and squeeze out all the moisture. Heat 1 to 2 tablespoons of the remaining oil. Add the zucchini and, over high heat, brown on all sides for 3 to 4 minutes; cook in two batches, adding more oil if necessary, if the zucchini pieces are too many for one pan. They should be softened but not mushy. Remove and set aside.

Drain the pasta, reserving ½ to ¾ cup of the cooking water. Remove 1 cup of the pasta sauce from its pan and warm the remainder. Add the pasta and reserved pasta water to the sauce in the pan and toss well. Add the zucchini and mozzarella and stir well.

Spoon the pasta mixture into the prepared casserole pan. Pour the reserved sauce over the top and sprinkle with the remaining bread crumbs and the Romano. Cover the casserole tightly with aluminum foil, and bake in the center of the oven for about 10 minutes, until warmed through. Remove the foil, check that the mozzarella is melted, and broil for 1 to 2 minutes to crisp the top before serving.

$\mathcal{L}$inguine with Red Clam Sauce

LINGUINE CON LE VONGOLE

There is clam sauce and there is clam sauce—and then there is this sauce.
You'll be surprised and seduced by the simple charms of this dish.

SERVES 4 TO 6

2 tablespoons olive oil

6 cloves garlic, thickly sliced

¼ teaspoon red pepper flakes

1 cup diced onion

1 28-ounce can whole peeled tomatoes,
    chopped and drained, juices reserved

¼ teaspoon salt

¼ teaspoon freshly ground black pepper

1 cup white wine

2 dozen littleneck or manila clams, well
    scrubbed

1 cup clam juice or Chicken Stock (page 223)

½ cup chopped fresh Italian parsley, plus
    additional for garnish

1 pound linguine

Bring a large pot of salted water to a boil.

In a wide, deep sauté pan, heat the oil over medium-high heat. Add the garlic, red pepper flakes, and onion, and sauté for 5 to 7 minutes, until the onion is well softened. Add the tomatoes, salt, and pepper. Cook for 4 to 6 minutes, until the mixture begins to look dry. Add the wine and clams. Increase the heat, cover the pan, and cook for 6 to 9 minutes, until the clams open. Peek after 5 to 6 minutes.

Uncover the pan, reduce the heat to medium-high, and remove the clams to a bowl. Discard any clams that have not opened. Cook the liquid in the pan for 2 to 3 minutes, uncovered. Add the clam juice or stock and 1 cup of the reserved tomato juice. Bring to a boil, reduce the heat, and cook for 20 to 25 minutes. Stir in the parsley and turn the heat to very low.

continued

Cook the linguine in the boiling water according to the package directions. Drain, and return the pasta to the cooking pot. Add half the sauce and toss well.

Add the cooked clams to the remaining sauce in the sauté pan. Stir and warm well. Divide the coated pasta into 4 or 6 equal portions. Top each with an equal amount of the sauce and clams. Sprinkle parsley over each portion and serve.

$\mathcal{P}$asta with Mortadella Sauce

PASTA DEI FRATI

In the olden days, most mortadella was made by monks, or frati, *in the hills of Emilia-Romagna. While mortadella is perhaps the least appreciated of Italian deli meats, it shines in this traditional sauce that I have updated.*

SERVES 6

1 28-ounce can Italian-style whole peeled tomatoes (preferably San Marzano), drained, juice reserved

2 tablespoons olive oil

6 cloves garlic, thickly sliced

¼ teaspoon red pepper flakes

¾ cup diced onion

8 ounces mortadella or bologna, cut into ½-inch dice (see Chef's Tip)

1½ cups whole milk

½ teaspoon salt, or to taste

½ teaspoon sugar, or to taste

4 tablespoons freshly grated Parmesan cheese, plus additional for the table

1 pound penne

1 to 2 tablespoons chopped fresh Italian parsley

Bring a large pot of salted water to a boil.

Break the tomatoes open to release more juice to be reserved. Chop the tomatoes and set aside; you should have about 1 heaping cup.

In a large deep sauté pan, combine the oil, garlic, red pepper flakes, and onion. Cook, stirring, over medium-high heat for 2 to 3 minutes. Add the mortadella and sauté, stirring, 5 to 7 minutes, until the mortadella browns. Add the chopped tomato and sauté for 1 to 2 minutes. Add 1½ cups of the reserved tomato juices, reduce the heat slightly, and simmer for 2 to 3 minutes. Add the milk and simmer until the mixture reaches a sauce consistency, about 15 to 20 minutes.

When the sauce is ready, taste, and add the salt and sugar if necessary. Stir well and simmer 2 to 3 minutes, and stir in the 4 tablespoons Parmesan.

continued

PASTA

Cook the pasta in the boiling water according to the package directions. Drain, and return to the cooking pot. Pour the sauce over the pasta and simmer over low heat, stirring constantly so the pasta is well coated, for 2 to 3 minutes. Serve immediately, sprinkled with the parsley. Pass Parmesan at the table.

Chef's Tip: *It might be easier to find domestic bologna at your local store, but I urge you to look for Italian mortadella, which has only recently been approved for importation into this country. The search will be well worth your while.*

$\mathscr{P}$asta with Prosciutto-and-Vegetable Sauce

PASTA CON PROSCIUTTO E VERDURE

Mothers all over the world know how difficult it is to persuade their children to eat their vegetables. My mother had some pretty creative ways of tricking my brother and me, and this sauce was one of her most successful.

SERVES 6

1 small leek

5 tablespoons olive oil

¼ cup finely diced carrot

¼ cup finely diced celery

1 cup sliced red bell pepper, cut into
    1-to-2-inch-long thin strips

1 cup peeled and diced eggplant, cut into
    ½-inch pieces

1 cup diced zucchini, cut into ½-inch pieces

¼ teaspoon freshly ground black pepper

6 cloves garlic, thickly sliced

4 ounces prosciutto or ham, cut into thin
    matchsticks or ¼-inch dice

¼ teaspoon red pepper flakes

1 28-ounce can of whole peeled tomatoes,
    drained and coarsely chopped, juice
    reserved

¾ cup Chicken Stock (page 223)

1 teaspoon dried oregano

½ teaspoon dried marjoram

¼ teaspoon sugar

½ cup frozen peas

¼ cup chopped fresh Italian parsley,
    plus 4 to 6 tablespoons for garnish

2 tablespoons sliced fresh basil leaves

2 teaspoons finely chopped fresh rosemary

¼ cup heavy cream (optional)

4 tablespoons freshly grated Parmesan cheese,
    plus additional for the table

1 pound farfalle or fusilli

Bring a large pot of salted water to a boil.

Cut the top off the leek, leaving the bottom 4 to 5 inches. Quarter lengthwise and soak in a bowl of cold water. Remove from the water and dry well. Cut off and discard the root ends. Thinly slice the leek crosswise.

In a large, deep sauté pan, heat 2 tablespoons of the oil over medium-high heat. Add the leek, carrot, and celery and sauté until they begin to soften, about 2 to 3 minutes. Add 2 tablespoons oil and the bell pepper, eggplant, zucchini, and black pepper. Increase the heat to high, and

continued

P A S T A

sauté the vegetables until they just begin to brown, about 3 to 5 minutes. The pan should not be overcrowded with vegetables. If there is more than one layer, the vegetables will steam instead of browning. When the vegetables have browned, remove and set aside.

Reduce the heat to medium-high. Add 1 tablespoon oil, and the garlic and prosciutto or ham, and sauté until the prosciutto or ham is lightly browned, about 2 to 4 minutes. Add the tomatoes and continue to cook until they become drier, about 4 to 6 minutes. Add the stock, 1½ cups of the reserved tomato juice, and the oregano, marjoram, and sugar.

Bring the sauce to a boil; simmer for 6 to 8 minutes. Add the reserved vegetables, peas, fresh herbs, and cream, if desired. Simmer for 7 to 8 minutes.

Cook the pasta in the boiling water according to the package directions. Drain, and return to the cooking pot. Pour the sauce over the pasta and simmer over low heat, stirring constantly, so the pasta is well coated, for 2 to 3 minutes. Add the 4 tablespoons Parmesan, stir well, and serve, sprinkled with more Parmesan and parsley.

Pasta with Ricotta-and-Saffron Sauce

PASTA AL SUGO DEL DOGE

The doges were the supreme rulers of the Venetian maritime republic. This most powerful city-state maintained trading routes to the Orient, importing exotic spices, among other goods. Saffron was a luxury, and cooking with it a way to display one's wealth. Here the spice of kings is used alongside ricotta, a peasant cheese.

SERVES 4 TO 6

2 tablespoons olive oil

6 ounces soppressata or salami, very finely diced

1 small onion, finely diced

8 cloves garlic, thickly sliced

Pinch red pepper flakes

¾ cup white wine

1¾ cups Chicken Stock (page 223), 2 teaspoons reserved

¼ teaspoon saffron powder, or ½ teaspoon finely crushed saffron threads (see Chef's Tip)

1 cup ricotta cheese

¾ cup freshly grated Parmesan cheese, plus additional for the table

¼ cup chopped fresh Italian parsley, plus additional for garnish

1 pound penne

Bring a large pot of salted water to a boil.

In a large, deep sauté pan, heat the oil over medium-high heat. Add the soppressata or salami and sauté for 1 to 2 minutes. Add the onion, garlic, and red pepper flakes, and sauté for 4 to 5 minutes. Add the wine, stir, and cook for 5 to 6 minutes, until most of the liquid is absorbed. Add all but the 2 teaspoons reserved stock and simmer for 12 to 15 minutes. Reduce the heat to very low.

While the sauce is simmering, in a separate bowl combine the saffron with the reserved stock. Add the ricotta, Parmesan, and ¼ cup parsley, and combine well; the mixture should be a bright yellow. Set aside.

Cook the pasta in the boiling water according to the package directions. Drain,

continued

and add the pasta to the sauce. Increase the heat to medium, toss well, and cook for 1 minute. Add the cheese mixture, toss, and cook for another 2 minutes, so the pasta is fully coated and creamy. Serve immediately, with more Parmesan and parsley.

Chef's Tip: *If saffron is too expensive for your budget, you may cheat by using turmeric. The flavor will not be exactly the same, but it will do.*

$\mathscr{S}$wordfish Picchio Pacchio Pasta

PASTA AL PICCHIO PACCHIO CON PESCESPADA

Picchio pacchio (pronounced "pick-yo pahk-yo") is my mother's name for picchipacchio, *a Sicilian tomato and onion sauce. My father elevates it by adding swordfish. This recipe requires up to 2 hours' marinating time, so plan accordingly.*

SERVES 6

2 28-ounce cans Italian-style whole peeled tomatoes (preferably San Marzano), drained, juice reserved

3 large fresh basil leaves, plus additional for garnish

2 teaspoons salt

½ teaspoon freshly ground black pepper

½ teaspoon sugar

¼ teaspoon dried oregano

½ teaspoon finely minced garlic, plus 2 cloves thickly sliced

2 pinches red pepper flakes

⅓ cup plus 5 tablespoons olive oil

½ cup all-purpose flour

½ teaspoon paprika

¾ pound fresh swordfish, cut into ½-inch cubes

½ cup finely chopped onion

½ cup white wine

1 pound spaghetti or linguine

With your hands or the back of a spoon, squeeze the tomatoes to release any remaining juice, and break them into medium pieces. Add the basil, 1 teaspoon of the salt, ¼ teaspoon of the pepper, the sugar, oregano, minced garlic, and 1 pinch red pepper flakes, and stir well. Add ⅓ cup of the reserved tomato juices and ⅓ cup of the oil, and stir well. Cover and let the flavors marinate for 1 to 2 hours.

Toward the end of that time, bring a large pot of salted water to a boil. Combine the flour, paprika, and remaining salt and pepper in a bowl large enough to hold the fish. Toss the cubes of fish in the flour mixture, and shake off the excess flour. Heat 3 tablespoons of the remaining oil in a medium saucepan over medium-high heat. Add the floured fish and sauté for

continued

PASTA

3 to 4 minutes, until lightly browned. Remove with a slotted spoon and set aside.

Reduce the heat to medium and add the remaining 2 tablespoons oil. Add the onion, sliced garlic, and remaining red pepper flakes. Cook until the onion is soft and browned, 2 to 3 minutes.

Increase the heat to medium–high and return the fish to the pan. Add the wine, scraping up any browned bits from the bottom of the pan, and stir gently to coat the fish well. The liquid should form a glaze over the fish-and-onion mixture. Turn off the heat and spoon the contents of the pan into the bowl with the marinade. Combine well.

Cook the pasta in the boiling water according to the package directions. Drain, and return to the cooking pot. Pour the sauce over the pasta and stir so that the pasta is well coated. (This is not meant to be a hot sauce.) Garnish with sliced or chopped basil leaves and serve.

Pasta with Pecorino and Salami

PASTA AL SUGO PECORINO

My wife and I tasted this dish in a small roadside trattoria between Rome and Montalcino, in Tuscany. The waiter was rude, the wine tasted like water, and we had to wait forever for the food. But once it arrived, it made us forgive everyone and forget everything.

SERVES 4 TO 6

4 tablespoons olive oil

1 cup chopped onion

5 large cloves garlic, thickly sliced

¼ teaspoon red pepper flakes

8 ounces salami, cut into ¼-inch dice

½ cup white wine

1½ cups Chicken Stock (page 223)

1 cup heavy cream

½ teaspoon freshly ground black pepper, plus additional for garnish

1 pound penne, ziti, or orecchiette

4 ounces freshly grated Romano cheese

Bring a large pot of salted water to a boil.

Heat the oil in a large skillet or sauté pan over medium-high heat. Add the onion, garlic, and red pepper flakes, and sauté until the onion is tender, 5 to 6 minutes. Add the salami and cook for 2 to 3 minutes. Pour in the wine, stir, and reduce the liquid by half, simmering for about 2 minutes. Add the stock, cream, and ½ teaspoon pepper. Bring the sauce to a boil, reduce the heat to medium, and simmer until thickened to a sauce consistency, about 15 minutes.

While the sauce is reducing, cook the pasta in the boiling water according to package directions. Drain, and return the pasta to the cooking pot. Stir the cheese into the sauce and cook until just melted. Pour the sauce over the pasta and simmer over low heat, stirring constantly, until the pasta is well coated, 1 to 2 minutes. Remove the pan from the heat and turn the pasta out onto a warm serving dish. Sprinkle with additional pepper and serve.

Pasta Boats

BARCHETTE DI PASTA

There are many versions of this dish in southern Italy. This is my personal interpretation, and like the others, it tastes great.

SERVES 6

3 eggplants (¾ to 1 pound), cut in half lengthwise

Salt, as needed

4 tablespoons olive oil, plus additional for brushing the eggplant

4 large cloves garlic, thickly sliced

2 tablespoons chopped fresh Italian parsley

4 ounces salami, chopped

¾ cup halved pitted black olives

¼ cup capers, rinsed

1 teaspoon anchovy paste (optional)

½ teaspoon freshly ground black pepper

1 recipe Spicy Tomato Sauce (page 230)

1 pound ditalini, penne lisce, penne rigate, or ziti

8 ounces fresh or smoked mozzarella or scamorza, cut into ¼-inch dice (see Chef's Tip)

⅓ cup freshly grated Romano cheese, plus more for the table

2 tablespoons Italian-Style Bread Crumbs (page 220)

Preheat the oven to 450°.

Lightly score the cut side of the eggplants and sprinkle with salt. Turn the pieces cut side down on paper towels and let the bitter juices drain for 15 to 20 minutes. Wipe the eggplants dry, brush with a little oil, and place cut side down on a baking sheet. Roast for 15 minutes, until the flesh is tender but not completely soft. They are done when the skins wrinkle slightly and when gentle pressure creates a dent that hold its shape. Remove from the oven, and when the eggplants are cool enough to handle, scoop out the tender flesh with a spoon, leaving a ½-inch-thick skin to use as a sturdy "boat." Chop the flesh for the filling.

Bring a large pot of salted water to a boil. Heat the 4 tablespoons of olive oil in a large skillet or sauté pan over medium-high heat. Add the garlic and parsley, and sauté until the garlic is golden, about

1 minute. Add the salami and eggplant flesh, and cook for 4 to 5 minutes, until the eggplant browns slightly. Stir in the olives, capers, anchovy paste if desired, pepper, and Spicy Tomato Sauce, and bring to a boil. Reduce the heat and simmer to a thick sauce consistency, 5 to 7 minutes.

Meanwhile, cook the pasta in the boiling water according to the package directions. Drain well, return to the cooking pot, and mix with half the sauce. Stir in the mozzarella or scamorza. Carefully spoon equal portions of the pasta mixture into the eggplant boats. Sprinkle the tops with the Romano and bread crumbs.

Bake on a lightly oiled baking sheet for 10 minutes, until warmed through and golden brown on top. Serve one pasta boat per person, with the extra sauce and additional Romano passed at the table.

Chef's Tip: *If using fresh mozzarella that was packed in water, drain on paper towels before dicing.*

Pasta with Beet, Sausage, and Gorgonzola Sauce

PASTA AL SUGO DI RAPE ROSSE, SALSICCIA E GORGONZOLA

I enjoyed a version of this dish, without the sausage, in the northern Trentino—Alto Adige region. My rendition includes sausage.

SERVES 4 TO 6

2 tablespoons olive oil

1 pound Italian-style sausage, casing removed

¼ cup chopped onion

6 large cloves garlic, thickly sliced

1 tablespoon chopped fresh sage (optional)

½ cup white wine

1 14-ounce can diced beets, drained
    (see Chef's Tips)

1 cup heavy cream

1 cup Beef Stock (page 221)

½ teaspoon salt

½ teaspoon freshly ground black pepper

1 pound butterfly, orecchiette, penne, or
    tortiglioni

½ cup crumbled Gorgonzola cheese

½ cup chopped toasted walnuts
    (see Chef's Tips)

2 tablespoons chopped fresh Italian parsley

Bring a large pot of salted water to a boil.

Heat the oil in a large skillet or saucepan over medium-high heat. Brown the sausage in the oil until it is cooked through, 5 to 6 minutes, breaking up the meat with a wooden spoon as it cooks. Remove from the pan and set aside.

Pour out all but 2 to 3 tablespoons excess fat from the pan. In the same pan, sauté the onion and garlic until tender, 4 to 5 minutes. Return the sausage to the pan, add the sage if desired, and stir well. Deglaze the pan with the wine, stirring to dislodge any browned bits from the bottom, and continue cooking to reduce the liquid by half, 1 to 2 minutes. Add the beets, cream, stock, salt and pepper. Bring the sauce to a boil, reduce the heat, and simmer for 10 to 12 minutes, until the mixture thickens to a sauce consistency. Meanwhile, cook the pasta in the boiling water according to the package directions. Drain well, and return to the cooking pot. Add the sauce and Gorgonzola and cook over low heat, stirring gently, until the cheese is melted and the sauce and pasta are thoroughly combined, 1 to 2 minutes. Serve on a warmed platter, sprinkled with the walnuts and parsley.

Chef's Tips: *If you want to use fresh beets, roast or boil 1 pound of them, skin and dice, and substitute for the canned.*

To toast walnuts, toss in a little olive oil and bake on a nonstick baking sheet in a preheated 325° oven for 5 to 6 minutes.

Pasta with Pancetta, Clams, and Mushrooms

PASTA CON PANCETTA, VONGOLE E FUNGHI

This is what happens when you are alone in the kitchen with no one telling you what to do. While making a plain sauce with clams, I found some mushrooms in the refrigerator. I threw them in, together with some pancetta, and liked the result so much that I added it to my pasta repertoire. Sometimes it pays to take chances.

SERVES 4 TO 6

4 tablespoons olive oil

4 ounces pancetta, thickly sliced and cut into ¼-inch dice, or bacon, cut into small pieces

½ cup chopped onion

6 large cloves garlic, thickly sliced

¼ teaspoon red pepper flakes

¼ pound shiitake mushrooms, stemmed and sliced

1½ pounds small clams, well scrubbed

½ cup white wine

1 cup clam juice or Chicken Stock (page 223)

½ cup Tomato Sauce (page 229)

½ cup heavy cream

½ teaspoon salt

½ teaspoon freshly ground black pepper

1 pound linguine

2 tablespoons chopped fresh Italian parsley

Bring a large pot of salted water to a boil.

Heat the oil in a large skillet or sauté pan over medium-high heat. Add the pancetta or bacon, and cook until crisp and brown, 2 minutes. Transfer to paper towels to drain.

In the same pan, sauté the onion, garlic, and red pepper flakes until the garlic is golden brown, 1 to 2 minutes. Add the mushrooms and cook over medium-high heat until the mushrooms have browned and the onions are tender, 4 to 6 minutes. Add the clams and wine, and stir well. Simmer the mixture over medium-high heat and remove the clams as they open. Discard any clams that have not opened after 4 minutes. Stir in the clam juice or stock, Tomato Sauce, cream, salt, and pepper, and bring the sauce to a boil. Reduce the heat to medium and simmer to a sauce consistency, 10 to 12 minutes.

Meanwhile, cook the pasta in the boiling water according to package directions. Drain, and return to the cooking pot. Pour on the sauce, clams, and pancetta or bacon. Toss together over low heat until the pasta and sauce are well combined, 1 to 2 minutes. Stir in the parsley and serve.

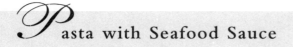

Pasta with Seafood Sauce

PASTA AL SUGO DI MARE

*Here is a sophisticated seafood sauce your friends and family will ask for
again and again.*

SERVES 4 TO 6

5 tablespoons olive oil

½ pound sea scallops, halved

½ pound uncooked medium shrimp, peeled
    and deveined

½ cup chopped onion

6 large cloves garlic, thickly sliced

2 tablespoons chopped fresh Italian parsley,
    plus additional for garnish

1 tablespoon freshly grated lemon zest

¼ teaspoon red pepper flakes

½ teaspoon curry powder

½ cup white wine

½ pound clams, well scrubbed

½ pound mussels, debearded and well
    scrubbed

1 cup clam juice or Chicken Stock (page 223)

½ cup Tomato Sauce (page 229)

½ teaspoon salt

½ teaspoon freshly ground black pepper

1 pound linguine

Bring a large pot of salted water to a boil.

Heat the oil in a large skillet or sauté pan
over medium–high to high heat. Sear the
scallops until just brown on both sides,
about 1 minute. Removed from the pan
and set aside. Sear the shrimp until just
pink but not cooked through, 30 seconds.
Remove and set aside with the scallops.

Reduce the heat to medium, add the
onions, garlic, parsley, lemon zest, and red
pepper flakes, and cook until the garlic
starts to brown, 3 to 4 minutes. Stir in the
curry powder and cook 1 minute more.
Add the wine, stirring well to dislodge any
browned bits from the bottom of the pan,
and simmer to reduce the wine by half,
2 minutes. Add the clams, mussels, clam
juice or stock, Tomato Sauce, salt, and
pepper, and bring the sauce to a boil. As
the clams and mussels open, remove them
from the sauce and set aside with the
shrimp and scallops. Discard any shellfish

that does not open after 4 minutes. Simmer the sauce until it has thickened slightly, 6 to 8 minutes.

Meanwhile, cook the linguine in the boiling water according to the package directions. When the pasta is just tender, drain and return to the cooking pot. Add the shellfish and sauce to the pasta and toss gently over low heat for 2 minutes to finish the cooking and combine all the ingredients. Serve hot, with additional parsley sprinkled on top.

$\mathscr{P}$asta with Shrimp Sauce

PASTA AL RAGÙ DI GAMBERETTI

I ate a version of this dish at a small trattoria in Rome. It was hot and humid outside, I was in a very bad mood, and my feet hurt from walking all morning. After a couple of bites I forgot all about my discomfort. Even now, when I make this dish at home, it works its restorative powers.

SERVES 4 TO 6

4 tablespoons olive oil

6 large cloves garlic, thickly sliced

¼ teaspoon red pepper flakes

3 tablespoons chopped fresh Italian parsley

1 28-ounce can Italian-style whole peeled tomatoes, drained and chopped, juice reserved

Pinch sugar, if needed

1 cup clam juice

½ cup all-purpose flour

1 teaspoon paprika

½ teaspoon salt, plus additional to taste

¼ teaspoon freshly ground black pepper, plus additional to taste

1 pound uncooked medium shrimp, peeled and deveined (see Chef's Tip)

½ cup white wine

1 pound linguine or spaghetti

Bring a large pot of salted water to a boil.

Heat half the oil in a skillet or saucepan over medium heat. Add the garlic, red pepper flakes, and 2 tablespoons of the parsley, and cook until the garlic is golden brown, about 1 minute. Add the tomatoes, and sugar if the tomatoes are tart. Simmer until most of the liquid has evaporated, about 4 to 5 minutes. Add the clam juice and reserved tomato juice. Bring the sauce to a boil and simmer until nice and thick, 12 to 15 minutes.

In a shallow bowl or on a plate, combine the flour, paprika, ½ teaspoon salt, and ¼ teaspoon pepper. Heat the remaining oil in a sauté pan or skillet over medium-high heat. Toss the shrimp in the flour mixture and fry them in the hot oil for 1 to 2 minutes on each side, until crisp and golden brown but not completely

Passione

cooked through. Add the wine, stirring to dislodge any browned bits from the bottom of the pan, and simmer to thicken the sauce and reduce the liquid by half, about 2 minutes. Pour the sauce over the shrimp and stir well to combine the flavors. Season with additional salt and pepper, if desired.

Cook the pasta in the boiling water according to package directions. Drain well, and return to the cooking pot. Add the shrimp sauce to the drained pasta and cook over low heat, stirring constantly, until the pasta and sauce have combined well, 1 to 2 minutes. Serve on a warmed platter, sprinkled with the remaining parsley.

Chef's Tip: *You might want to experiment with different types of shrimp, as they have different textures and handle the heat in different ways. Rock shrimp are fairly resilient, which makes them ideal for this recipe. Stay away from precooked shrimp, which will overcook to a rubbery consistency.*

Pasta with Spinach, Gorgonzola, and Prosciutto Sauce

PASTA AL SUGO DI SPINACI, GORGONZOLA E PROSCIUTTO

This elegant sauce goes well with any kind of pasta, especially tortellini, and with gnocchi. It is very rich, and thus best saved for special occasions.

SERVES 4 TO 6

1 10-ounce box frozen spinach, thawed, or 1 large bunch fresh spinach, blanched

4 tablespoons olive oil

4 large cloves garlic, thickly sliced

½ cup white wine

1 cup Chicken Stock (page 223)

1 cup heavy cream

¼ teaspoon freshly ground black pepper

4 ounces prosciutto or ham, thinly sliced and cut into ribbons

½ cup crumbled Gorgonzola cheese

1 pound penne rigate, ziti, or tortiglioni

¼ cup freshly grated Parmesan cheese

Bring a large pot of salted water to a boil. Drain the spinach of excess moisture by pressing the leaves between two plates or squeezing by hand.

Heat 3 tablespoons of the oil in a large sauté pan or skillet over medium-high heat, and gently cook the garlic until golden brown, about 1 minute. Add the spinach and cook 1 minute. Add the wine and simmer to reduce the liquid by half, about 2 minutes. Add the stock, cream, and pepper. Bring the liquid to a boil, reduce the heat, and simmer to a sauce consistency, 10 to 12 minutes. Cool the sauce slightly, pour into a blender, and process to a smooth cream.

In a sauté pan over medium-high heat, fry the prosciutto or ham in the remaining oil until it is crisp and brown, about 3 minutes. Scoop out of the pan and drain on paper towels. Pour the spinach sauce into the same pan, stir in the Gorgonzola, and warm gently until the cheese has melted, 1 to 2 minutes.

Cook the pasta in the boiling water according to the package directions. Drain, and return to the cooking pot. Pour the spinach sauce over the pasta and simmer over low heat, stirring constantly, until the pasta is well coated, 1 to 2 minutes. Remove from the heat and turn the pasta out onto a warmed serving dish. Sprinkle with the crisp prosciutto or ham and Parmesan, and serve.

Fresh Pasta

inally the secret is out. Making fresh pasta is simpler than you may have imagined. Mind you, the first few tries may be a bit difficult, but the basic recipe is easy to master, and of course, practice makes perfect.

I recommend that the first time you attempt any of the recipes in this chapter, you make a "large" batch. (I have included recipes for three yields, small, medium, and large.) You will be working with probably more amounts of ingredients than you need, but the extra will allow you a wide margin of error. You might then end up with more pasta dough than you need; if, like me, though, you are prone to mistakes, this small inconvenience will turn to your advantage.

I prefer to use a hand-crank machine for making fresh pasta, as it allows more control overall and results in a better finish to the pasta. I shy away from electric machines that produce only pasta shapes, not pasta sheets. As far as the pasta-making attachments designed for heavy-duty kitchen mixers, some of these are good alternatives to hand-crank machines.

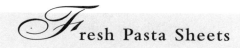

Fresh Pasta Sheets

PASTA FRESCA

Large Batch

Use this for tortellini, ravioli, and half-moon recipes unless instructed otherwise.

MAKES 12 15-INCH SHEETS
(ABOUT 1 1/4 POUNDS)

3 to 3½ cups all-purpose flour, plus additional as needed

5 large eggs

2 tablespoons olive oil

½ teaspoon salt

Sift the flour onto a clean countertop or into a large bowl. Make a deep well in the center.

In a small bowl, beat together the eggs, oil, and salt. Pour this mixture into the well. With a fork, gradually beat the flour into the liquid to make a smooth paste. Continue mixing until you have a firm dough. Knead the dough, adding more flour as needed, to form a strong, smooth, elastic ball. You may not use all of the flour, or you may need to add more. The kneading process should take 4 to 5 minutes. Cover the dough with a clean kitchen towel and let rest for 5 to 10 minutes.

To make pasta sheets, use a roller-style machine. Cut the dough into 6 equal pieces. Work with one piece at a time, leaving the remaining pieces covered. Dust the first piece with flour and run it through the machine with the rollers adjusted to the thickest setting (commonly numbered 1). Fold the dough in thirds and press gently. Feed the narrow edge into the roller, and run the dough through the machine once more.

Adjust the rollers to the next-smaller setting (commonly numbered 2), and roll the narrower end of the dough through the machine. Dust lightly with flour if the dough is sticky. Continue altering the setting by one notch and rolling the dough through to form a long sheet. Dust with

continued

P A S T A

additional flour as needed. I tend not to use the thinnest setting (7), as it makes pasta too thin for most dishes. Cut the sheet in half for easier handling.

Place the sheets on a well-floured surface or clean, lint-free cloth, and continue the rolling process with the remaining pieces of dough. Use the sheets for lasagna or cannelloni, or stuff them to make ravioli or tortelloni. Or run the sheets through the cutter to make linguine or fettuccine.

Medium Batch

Use this for all lasagna and layered recipes unless instructed otherwise.

MAKES 10 15-INCH SHEETS
(ABOUT 1 1/4 POUNDS)

2½ cups all-purpose flour, plus additional
    as needed

4 large eggs

½ teaspoon salt

1½ tablespoons olive oil

Follow the instructions for the Large Batch (page 39). Cut the kneaded dough into 5 (rather than 6) equal pieces.

Small Batch

Use this for lasagnette and medallion recipes unless instructed otherwise.

MAKES 8 15-INCH SHEETS
(ABOUT 1 POUND)

2 cups all-purpose flour, plus additional
    as needed

3 large eggs

¼ teaspoon salt

1 tablespoon olive oil

Follow the instructions for the Large Batch (page 39). Cut the kneaded dough into 4 (rather than 6) equal pieces.

 Green Lasagna with Pine Nuts, Ricotta, and Stewed Garlic

Pappardelle with Rustic Lamb Sauce

 Meat Tortellini with Garlic Cream Sauce

Swordfish Picchio Pacchio Pasta

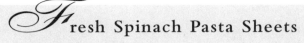resh Spinach Pasta Sheets

PASTA FRESCA AGLI SPINACI

MAKES 12 15-INCH SHEETS
(ABOUT 1 1/4 POUNDS)

¼ cup cooked spinach, squeezed very dry

2 tablespoons olive oil

4 large eggs

3 to 3½ cups all-purpose flour, plus additional as needed

½ teaspoon salt

Purée the spinach, oil, and 1 egg to a smooth paste in a blender or food processor.

Sift the flour onto a clean countertop or into a large bowl. Make a deep well in the center. In a small bowl, beat together the spinach purée, remaining eggs, and salt. Pour this mixture into the well. With a fork, gradually beat the flour into the liquid to make a smooth paste. Continue mixing until you have a firm dough. Knead the dough, adding more flour as needed, to form a strong, smooth, elastic ball. You may not use all of the flour, or you may need to add more. The kneading process should take 4 to 5 minutes. Cover the dough with a clean kitchen towel and let rest for 5 to 10 minutes.

To make the pasta sheets, use a roller-style machine. Cut the dough into 6 equal pieces. Work with one piece at a time, leaving the remaining pieces covered. Dust the first piece of dough with flour and run it through the machine with the rollers adjusted to the thickest setting (commonly numbered 1). Fold the dough over onto itself, press, and roll again. Dust lightly with flour if the dough is sticky. Adjust the rollers to the next-smaller setting (commonly numbered 2), and roll the narrower end of the dough through the machine. Continue altering the setting by one notch and rolling the dough through to form a long sheet. Dust with additional flour as needed. I tend not to use the final, thinnest setting (7), as it makes pasta too thin for most dishes. Cut the sheet in half for easier handling.

Place the finished sheets on a well-floured surface or clean, lint-free cloth, and continue the rolling process with the remaining pieces of dough. Use the sheets for lasagna or cannelloni, or stuff them to make ravioli or tortelloni. Or run the sheets through the cutter to make linguine or fettuccine.

PASTA

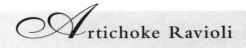rtichoke Ravioli

RAVIOLI DI CARCIOFI

Many people don't know the bounty of flavor hidden in the heart of the thorny leaves of an artichoke, but once they experience the taste, they will always come back for more.

SERVES 4 TO 6

3 large fresh artichokes (see Chef's Tip)

Juice of 1 lemon

4 tablespoons olive oil

1 cup thinly sliced onion

4 large cloves garlic, thickly sliced

2 tablespoons chopped fresh Italian parsley

⅛ teaspoon red pepper flakes

½ teaspoon dried thyme

¾ cup white wine

2 cups Chicken Stock (page 223)

½ teaspoon salt, plus additional to taste

½ teaspoon freshly ground black pepper, plus additional to taste

½ cup freshly grated Parmesan cheese, plus additional for garnish

1 whole egg

1 cup heavy cream

1 recipe Fresh Pasta Sheets, Large Batch (page 39)

1 egg yolk mixed with 1 tablespoon water

Flour for dusting

Prepare the artichokes: Pour the lemon juice into a large bowl of cold water. Rub your hands with the lemon rinds to keep your skin from being stained. Repeat this procedure for each artichoke: Pull back and snap off the first few layers of tough outer leaves. Turn the artichoke upside down, holding it by the leaf end. With a sharp paring knife and a circular motion, cut away the dark green peel from the stem area as you would the skin from an apple. To remove the thorny leaves, plunge the tip of a large chef's knife through them, about 2 to 2½ inches from the bottom of the artichoke. Slice the thorny tops of the leaves off at the cut mark. Cut the artichoke in quarters, and place them on a cutting board. For each quarter, put the point of the paring knife behind the last row of purplish leaves encasing the hairy choke. With a slow and steady motion, cut out the choke, being careful not to slice

Passione

off the tender heart. You now should have a fully trimmed artichoke quarter with no tough leaves or coarse center. Place the trimmed pieces in the bowl of lemon water until ready to use.

In a wide saucepan or a 12-inch skillet, combine oil, onion, garlic, parsley, red pepper flakes, and thyme. Cook for 10 to 12 minutes over medium heat, stirring every few minutes, until the onion and garlic are tender and golden brown. Increase the heat to high, add the artichokes, and cook, stirring well, for 2 to 3 minutes, until the artichokes start to brown slightly. Be careful not to burn the onion. Add the wine and cook for 2 to 3 minutes, stirring well to dislodge any browned bits from the bottom of the pan. Add the stock, and ½ teaspoon each salt and pepper, and bring to a boil. Stir, and reduce the heat to simmer, with the pan almost covered, until the artichokes are tender, 20 to 25 minutes.

Strain the mixture to collect the liquid, pressing the solids gently to release as much juice as possible. Return the liquid to the pan. In a food processor or blender, purée the solids with the ½ cup Parmesan and the egg to obtain a thick paste.

Add the cream to the cooking liquid and bring the mixture to a boil. Reduce the heat and simmer to a sauce consistency, 8 to 10 minutes. Season to taste with salt and pepper, and set aside.

To make ravioli, lay one sheet of pasta flat on a well-floured work surface. Drop teaspoonfuls of the artichoke filling on the pasta at 2-inch intervals. The spoonfuls are each the filling for individual ravioli, so make sure there is enough room between them to form and seal the pasta. Brush the egg-yolk-and-water mixture lightly around the spoonfuls of filling. Place another pasta sheet on top and gently press down around the mounds of filling with your fingers. Eliminate any excess air, or the ravioli may burst during cooking. Press more firmly to seal the layers, and cut the pasta into desired shapes with a wheel. Pull the ravioli apart and dust generously with flour to prevent them from sticking together. Place on a baking sheet or tray. Repeat the process with the remaining pasta sheets and filling. Cover the ravioli with plastic wrap and refrigerate until ready to cook. (They can be kept refrigerated for 1 day.)

continued

PASTA

Bring a large pot of salted water to a boil. Cook the ravioli in the boiling water until the fillings are heated through and the pasta is al dente, 3 to 4 minutes. Drain well, and distribute on warmed plates. Drizzle with the sauce and garnish with Parmesan and pepper if desired.

Chef's Tip: *If you can't find fresh artichokes, substitute 1½ cups thawed frozen artichoke hearts, or 1½ cups rinsed and drained canned.*

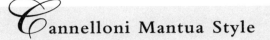Cannelloni Mantua Style

CANNELLONI MANTOVANI

The fortified city of Mantua, or Mantova, has a charm all its own. I had this dish there many years ago while traveling with my father. I particularly like the sauce, which can be used with any type of pasta.

SERVES   6

Olive oil as needed

1 recipe Fresh Pasta Sheets, Medium Batch (page 40), or 1 pound dry cannelloni or manicotti

8 ounces ricotta cheese

8 ounces fresh mozzarella cheese, cut into ¼-inch dice

1½ cups freshly grated Parmesan cheese, plus additional for garnish

4 ounces prosciutto or ham, finely chopped

2 eggs

2 tablespoons chopped fresh Italian parsley, plus additional for garnish

½ teaspoon freshly ground black pepper

1 recipe Tomato Sauce Mantua Style (page 231)

Bring a large pot of salted water to a boil. Lightly oil a 9x13-inch lasagna pan or baking dish. Cut the fresh pasta sheets into 5-inch squares. Fill a large bowl with ice water mixed with a few tablespoons of olive oil. Cook 3 or 4 fresh pasta squares at a time in the boiling water until al dente, about 1 minute. If you are using dry pasta, cook according to the package directions. Lift the cooked pasta from the pot and plunge directly into the ice water. Drain, and place flat on a lightly oiled baking sheet. If you are stacking the pasta or storing it for later use, brush or spray each of the pieces with oil to prevent them from sticking together. Cover the cooked pasta with plastic wrap until ready to use.

In a medium bowl, combine the ricotta, mozzarella, and 1½ cups Parmesan. Stir in the prosciutto, eggs, 2 tablespoons parsley, and pepper to form a thick filling. Set aside.

continued

PASTA

Preheat the oven to 425°. Spread half the tomato sauce on the bottom of the prepared lasagna pan. Spoon ¼ cup of the cheese filling onto the middle of each pasta square. Roll the pasta into fat cigars (they're now cannelloni, "little tubes") and place them seam side down on the tomato sauce in the pan. If you cooked dry pasta, fill each piece using a pastry bag or a long spoon. Drizzle the cannelloni with the remaining tomato sauce and sprinkle with Parmesan and parsley.

Bake until heated through and lightly browned, 20 to 25 minutes. Let rest for 5 minutes before serving.

$\mathscr{G}$reen Lasagna with Pine Nuts, Ricotta, and Stewed Garlic

LASAGNE VERDI CON PINOLI, RICOTTA E AGLIO BRASATO

This is a delightful change from traditional lasagna. The flavors are bound to appeal to the most sophisticated palates, but the soul of the dish lies in the simplicity of its ingredients and preparation.

SERVES 6 TO 8

⅓ cup olive oil, plus additional as needed

3 cups chopped onions

12 large cloves garlic, thickly sliced

¼ cup chopped fresh basil

½ teaspoon salt

½ teaspoon freshly ground black pepper

½ cup Marsala wine

2 cups Spicy Tomato Sauce (page 230)

1 recipe Fresh Spinach Pasta Sheets (page 41), or 1 pound dry spinach lasagna

2 cups ricotta cheese

2 eggs, separated

1 cup plus 2 tablespoons freshly grated Parmesan cheese

1 cup toasted pine nuts (see Chef's Tip)

2 tablespoons chopped fresh Italian parsley

Heat the oil in a large saucepan over medium heat. Stir in the onions and garlic, and cook 1 to 2 minutes, until they start to sizzle. Reduce the heat to low and simmer slowly, stirring often, until the onion is tender and brown, 25 to 30 minutes. Season with the basil, salt, and pepper. Add the Marsala, stirring to dislodge any browned bits from the bottom of the pan, and simmer over medium-high heat until the liquid is absorbed, 4 to 5 minutes. Add the Spicy Tomato Sauce and bring the mixture to a boil, stirring to combine the flavors. Remove the sauce from the heat and let cool to room temperature.

Bring a large pot of salted water to a boil. Fill a large bowl with ice water mixed with a few tablespoons of oil. Cook 3 or 4 pasta sheets at a time in the boiling water until al dente, about 1 minute. If you are

continued

using dry pasta, cook according to the package directions. Lift the cooked sheets out of the pot and plunge them directly into the ice water. Drain, and place flat on a lightly oiled baking sheet. If you are stacking the pasta or storing it for later use, brush or spray the sheets with oil so they do not stick together. Cover the cooked pasta with plastic wrap until ready to use.

In a medium bowl, combine the ricotta and egg yolks until creamy and smooth. Fold in one cup of the Parmesan. Whip the egg whites until soft peaks form, and fold into the ricotta mixture. Set aside.

Preheat the oven to 450°. To assemble the lasagna, line the bottom of a 9x13-inch lasagna pan or baking dish with 1 cup of the sauce. Place a layer of pasta on top of the sauce, trimming and overlapping the sheets to fit. Spread the pasta with ¾ cup of the ricotta mixture, sprinkle 2 to 3 tablespoons of the pine nuts, and spread ½ cup of the sauce. Top with another layer of pasta. Continue layering in this fashion with the remaining ingredients, finishing with the ricotta mixture and pine nuts.

Bake for 12 to 15 minutes, until the top is golden brown and bubbling. Let rest for 5 minutes, sprinkle with the chopped parsley and the remaining 2 tablespoons Parmesan, and serve.

Chef's Tip: *To toast pine nuts, toss them in a little olive oil and bake on a nonstick baking sheet in a preheated 325° oven for 5 to 6 minutes, until they are a light golden brown.*

Green Pansoti with Potatoes and Roasted Garlic

PANSOTI VERDI CON PATATE E AGLIO ARROSTITO

The word pansoti, *or "little tummies," describes perfectly the singular shape of this pasta.*

SERVES 4 TO 6

1 pound russet potatoes, well scrubbed

2 tablespoons roasted garlic pulp (see Chef's Tip page 251)

4 ounces salami, sliced and chopped into ¼-inch dice

1 whole egg

½ cup freshly grated Parmesan cheese, plus additional for the table

¼ teaspoon salt

¼ teaspoon freshly ground black pepper

1 recipe Fresh Spinach Pasta Sheets (page 41)

1 egg yolk mixed with 1 tablespoon water

Flour for dusting

2 cups Tomato Sauce (page 229), warmed

To make the filling, bake or boil the potatoes until tender. Cool slightly, remove the skins, and mash. In a medium bowl, combine the potatoes, garlic pulp, salami, egg, and ½ cup Parmesan. Season with salt and pepper.

Cut the pasta sheets into 2½-to-3-inch squares. Place a teaspoon of the filling in the center of each square, dab the sides with the egg-yolk-and-water mixture, and fold the squares over to form a triangle. Press out any excess air and pinch the edges to seal them. Place the finished pasta on a floured tray and dust with flour to prevent the pansoti from sticking together. Cover with plastic wrap and refrigerate until ready to use.

Bring a large pot of salted water to a boil. Cook the pasta in the boiling water until the filling is heated through and the pasta is tender, 2 to 3 minutes. Drain, and return to the cooking pot. Add the Tomato Sauce and toss gently over low heat until combined, 1 to 2 minutes. Serve hot and pass the Parmesan at the table.

PASTA

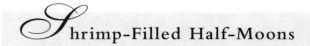

Shrimp-Filled Half-Moons

MEZZELUNE AL GAMBERO

These distinctively shaped fresh-pasta pillows are just as much fun to make as to eat.

SERVES 4 TO 6

¾ pound uncooked medium shrimp, peeled and deveined (use shells for Quick Shrimp Sauce)

2 tablespoons white wine

2 tablespoons heavy cream

1 tablespoon chopped green onion, white part only

1 whole egg

¼ teaspoon salt

¼ teaspoon freshly ground black pepper

1 egg yolk mixed with 1 tablespoon water

1 recipe Fresh Pasta Sheets, Large Batch (page 39)

Flour for dusting

1 recipe Quick Shrimp Sauce (page 250)

2 tablespoons chopped fresh Italian parsley

To make the filling, stir together the shrimp, wine, cream, and onion. Let marinate for at least 10 minutes. Add the egg, salt, and pepper, and process in a blender or food processor to obtain a thick paste.

Cut the pasta sheets with a cookie cutter into 2½-to-3-inch rounds. Spoon 1 tea-spoon of the shrimp filling on the top half of each round, dab the edges with the egg-yolk-and-water mixture, and fold the bottom half over the filling to form a half-moon. Press out any excess air and pinch the edges to seal them. Place the finished pasta on a floured tray and dust with flour to prevent the pieces from sticking together. Cover with plastic and refrigerate until ready to use.

Heat the Quick Shrimp Sauce in a saucepan. Bring a large pot of salted water to a boil, and cook the pasta in the boiling water until the filling is just cooked through and the pasta is tender, 2 to 3 minutes. Drain, and return to the cooking pot. Pour the sauce over the pasta and toss gently over low heat to combine, 1 to 2 minutes. Spoon the pasta and sauce onto a warmed serving platter and sprinkle with the parsley. Serve hot.

$\mathscr{Z}$ucchini-Filled Half-Moons with Roasted Garlic Sauce

MEZZELUNE DI ZUCCHINE CON SUGO ALL'AGLIO ARROSTITO

Garlic and zucchini are a marriage made in heaven. Once you have mastered the art of fresh pasta-making, you can use this filling for tortellini, ravioli, pansoti, or any other shape that strikes your fancy.

SERVES 4 TO 6

3 tablespoons olive oil

3 large cloves garlic, thickly sliced

⅛ teaspoon red pepper flakes

2 medium zucchini, grated

2 teaspoons chopped fresh basil, or 1 teaspoon dried

1½ teaspoons chopped fresh mint, or 1 teaspoon dried

½ teaspoon salt, plus additional to taste

½ teaspoon freshly ground black pepper, plus additional to taste

½ cup ricotta cheese

½ cup freshly grated Parmesan cheese, plus additional for garnish

1 whole egg

1 recipe Fresh Pasta Sheets, Large Batch (page 39)

1 egg yolk mixed with 1 tablespoon water

Flour for dusting

1 recipe Roasted Garlic Sauce (page 251)

Heat the oil in a large saucepan over medium-high heat. Stir in the garlic and red pepper flakes, and cook until the garlic is golden brown, 1 minute. Add the zucchini, basil, mint, and ½ teaspoon each salt and pepper, and stir to combine. Cook, stirring often, until the zucchini have softened completely and browned to intensify the flavor, 10 to 12 minutes. Cool to room temperature.

In a medium bowl, stir together the zucchini mixture, ricotta, Parmesan, and egg. Taste, and season with salt and pepper as desired.

To make the half-moons, cut the pasta sheets with a cookie cutter into 2½-to-3-inch rounds. Spoon 1 teaspoon of the zucchini filling onto the top half of each round, dab the edges with the egg-yolk-

continued

and-water mixture, and fold the bottom half over the filling to form a half-moon. Press out any excess air and pinch the edges to seal them. Place the finished pasta on a floured tray and dust with flour to prevent the pieces from sticking together. Cover with plastic wrap and refrigerate until ready to use.

Bring a large pot of salted water to a boil. Cook the pasta in the boiling water until the filling is heated through and the pasta is tender, 2 to 3 minutes. Drain, and return to the cooking pot. Add the Roasted Garlic Sauce and toss gently over low heat to combine, 1 to 2 minutes. Spoon the pasta and sauce onto a warmed serving platter, sprinkle with Parmesan, and serve.

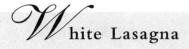

White Lasagna

LASAGNE IN BIANCO

Who says you can make lasagna only with red sauce? This recipe finds its roots in the Emilia-Romagna region of Italy. Surprise your friends with this unusual rendition.

SERVES 8

Olive oil as needed

1 recipe Fresh Pasta Sheets, Medium Batch (page 40), or 1 pound dry lasagna

1 recipe White Meat Sauce (page 227)

1½ cups freshly grated Parmesan cheese

1 recipe Parmesan Béchamel Sauce (see Chef's Tips page 235)

Preheat the oven to 450°. Lightly grease a 9x13-inch lasagna pan or baking dish.

Bring a large pot of salted water to a boil. Fill a large bowl with ice water mixed with a few tablespoons of olive oil. Cook 3 or 4 pasta sheets at a time in the boiling water until al dente, about 1 minute. If you are using dry lasagna, cook the pasta according to the package directions. Lift the cooked sheets out of the pot and plunge directly into the ice water. Drain, and place flat on a lightly oiled baking sheet. If you are stacking the sheets or storing for later use, brush or spray them with oil to prevent them from sticking together. Cover with plastic wrap until ready to use.

Cover the bottom of the lasagna pan with 1 cup of the White Meat Sauce. Cover the sauce with an even layer of cooked pasta, overlapping and trimming as needed. Spread 1 cup of meat sauce over the pasta, sprinkle with ½ cup of the Parmesan, and add another layer of pasta. Repeat with two more layers, ending with a layer of pasta. Spread the Parmesan Béchamel Sauce evenly over the top.

Bake for 15 to 20 minutes, until puffy and lightly browned. Allow to rest for 10 minutes before serving.

Lasagnette with Curried Shrimp and Scallops

LASAGNETTE DI GAMBERI E CAPESANTE AL CURRY

Lasagnette is a fairly loose term for smaller sheets of fresh pasta layered one atop another in a free form, usually between layers of sauces. This is my version of a dish I enjoyed in Lucca.

SERVES 6

1 tablespoon olive oil, plus additional
    as needed

1 recipe Fresh Pasta Sheets, Small Batch
    (page 40), or 4 to 6 dry lasagna noodles

1 tablespoon unsalted butter

¾ pound uncooked medium shrimp, peeled,
    deveined, and cut into ½-inch pieces

¾ pound small bay scallops

2 tablespoons brandy

¼ teaspoon salt

¼ teaspoon freshly ground pepper

1 recipe Curry Sauce (page 236)

Truffle oil (optional)

½ cup diced fresh tomato

1 tablespoon chopped fresh Italian parsley

Preheat the oven to 450°. Lightly butter 6 individual gratin dishes.

Bring a large pot of salted water to a boil. Fill a large bowl with ice water mixed with a few tablespoons of oil. Cut the fresh pasta sheets into pieces that fit neatly into the gratin dishes (4-inch squares for similar-size round dishes, or 3x5-inch rectangles for similar-size ovals). Cook the pasta squares, a few at a time, in the boiling water until al dente, about 1 minute. Scoop out the pasta and immediately plunge in the ice water. If you are using dry pasta, cook the whole pieces according to the package directions and cut them into the correct size and shape after they have cooked and cooled. Drain the pasta well and lay flat on a baking sheet or tray. If you are stacking the sheets or storing for later use, brush or spray them with oil to prevent them from sticking together. Cover with plastic wrap until ready to use.

Heat 1 tablespoon of oil and the butter in a large skillet or sauté pan over high heat. Toss in the shrimp and scallops and sear them quickly. After about 1½ minutes, when the shellfish is evenly opaque or lightly browned, but not fully cooked, add the brandy and stir to dislodge any browned bits from the bottom of the pan. Remove the pan from the heat, and season the shellfish with the salt and pepper. Be careful not to overcook the seafood, or it will be tough and dry in the finished dish.

To assemble the lasagnette, spoon 2 tablespoons Curry Sauce into the bottom of each gratin dish. Place a piece of pasta on top and cover with 2 heaping tablespoons of the seafood and juices. Drizzle with another tablespoon of sauce. Repeat with the remaining ingredients, finishing with a layer of pasta and the remaining sauce.

Bake the lasagnette for about 10 minutes, until lightly browned and bubbling. Remove from the oven and let rest for 5 minutes. Top each with 2 or 3 drops of truffle oil if desired, diced tomato, and a sprinkling of parsley. Serve at once.

$\mathcal{L}$obster Ravioli

RAVIOLI D'ARAGOSTA

This recipe is for special occasions. While it is not hard to assemble and prepare, it is time-consuming. If you are in a rush, save it for when you have some leisure. Like a languid kiss, it requires the full attention of body and soul. Anything less will not do.

SERVES 6

(MAKES ABOUT 36 1 1/2-INCH RAVIOLI)

SAUCE

2 1½-pound whole lobsters or
   3 8-to-10-ounce lobster tails, cooked

4 tablespoons unsalted butter

2 tablespoons olive oil

½ cup diced carrot

¾ cup diced onion

½ cup diced celery

1 bay leaf

6 large cloves garlic, thickly sliced

½ cup brandy

3 cups Chicken Stock (page 223)

1 cup heavy cream

Salt and freshly ground black pepper to taste

FILLING

½ cup heavy cream

2 tablespoons brandy

Reserved lobster meat

1 tablespoon chopped fresh Italian parsley

¼ teaspoon salt

¼ teaspoon freshly ground black pepper

1 egg white

1 recipe Fresh Pasta Sheets, Large Batch
   (page 39)

Flour as needed

1 egg yolk mixed with 1 tablespoon water

½ cup diced fresh tomato

4 tablespoons thinly sliced fresh basil

Separate the lobster meat from the shells, and reserve for the filling.

Make the sauce: In a large saucepan or stockpot, melt the butter with the oil over medium heat. Add the carrot, onion, celery, bay leaf, and garlic, and cook 1 to 2 minutes, until aromatic. Add the lobster shells, and sauté, stirring regularly, for 10 to 15 minutes, until the vegetables are tender and light brown. Add the brandy, stirring to dislodge any browned bits from the bottom of the pan, and simmer for 3 minutes, or until the liquid is reduced by half.

$\mathcal{P}assione$

Add the stock, bring the liquid to a boil, and reduce the heat and simmer, almost covered, for 1 hour. Strain the stock through a sieve or mesh strainer. Discard the solids and pour the strained stock into a saucepan. Add the cream, bring the liquid to a boil, and reduce the heat and simmer until the sauce is glossy and thick, about 35 to 40 minutes. Season to taste with salt and pepper; note that the sauce may already be quite salty from the lobster shells.

While the sauce is simmering (keep warm once it has simmered enough), make the filling: In a medium saucepan, combine the cream and brandy. Boil over medium-high heat until the liquid is reduced by half to a syrupy consistency, 3 to 4 minutes. Chop the lobster meat and stir into the cream mixture. Add the parsley, salt, and pepper. In a blender or food processor purée the mixture with the egg white to a smooth, thick paste. Refrigerate until ready to use.

To make the ravioli, lay one sheet of pasta flat on a well-floured work surface. Place teaspoonfuls of the filling on the pasta at 2-inch intervals. The spoonfuls will each be individual ravioli, so make sure there is enough room between them to form and seal the pasta. Brush the egg-yolk-and-water mixture lightly around the dropped spoonfuls. Cover with another pasta sheet and press down gently with your fingers. Eliminate any excess air in the ravioli, or they may burst during cooking. Press more firmly to seal the layers, and cut the pasta with a wheel to make the desired ravioli shapes. Pull the pieces apart and dust generously with flour. Place on a baking sheet or tray well dusted with flour. Repeat the process with the remaining pasta sheets and filling. Cover with plastic wrap and refrigerate until ready to use. (The filled pasta can be kept refrigerated for 1 day.)

Bring a large pot of salted water to a boil. Cook the ravioli in the water until al dente, 2 to 3 minutes. Drain well and distribute on individual plates. Spoon the warm lobster sauce on top, garnish with the tomato and basil, and serve.

$\mathcal{M}$eat Tortellini with Garlic Cream Sauce

TORTELLINI DI CARNE CON CREMA ALL'AGLIO

*This is not a dish for dieters—any fat-free substitutions would deprive it
of its decadent flavor. So, as I always say, exercise regularly, eat judiciously
the rest of the week, and on the weekend enjoy this delectable delicacy
without guilt.*

SERVES 4 TO 6

4 tablespoons olive oil

¼ cup diced celery

¼ cup diced carrot

¼ cup diced onion

4 large cloves garlic, thickly sliced

1 pound ground veal

1 ounce prosciutto or ham, chopped

½ cup white wine

1 cup Chicken Stock (page 223)

¼ teaspoon salt

¼ teaspoon freshly ground black pepper

1 whole egg

¼ cup freshly grated Parmesan cheese

2 tablespoons Italian-Style Bread Crumbs
     (page 220)

1 recipe Fresh Pasta Sheets, Large Batch
     (page 39)

1 egg yolk mixed with 1 tablespoon water

Flour as needed

1 recipe Garlic Cream Sauce (page 237),
     warmed

To make the filling, heat the oil over
medium heat in a large saucepan. Add the
celery, carrot, onion, and garlic, and sauté
slowly, until tender and golden brown,
5 to 6 minutes. Increase the heat to
medium-high and add the veal and
prosciutto or ham. Cook, stirring often,
until the meat starts to brown, 10 to 12
minutes. Add the wine, gently scraping
the bottom of the pan to dislodge any
browned bits, and cook until the liquid is
reduced by half, about 1 minute. Add the
stock and season with the salt and pepper.
Bring the mixture to a boil and simmer
until nearly dry, about 15 minutes. Cool
the mixture slightly, and in a food processor or blender purée with the egg, Parmesan, and bread crumbs to a thick paste.

To make the tortellini, cut the pasta sheets
into 2-inch squares. Place a teaspoon of
the filling in the center of each square and

fold it over to form a triangle. Press out any excess air and seal the edges with the egg-yolk-and-water mixture. Pull the corners of the longest side of the triangle around and pinch them together. Fold the remaining tip up to form individual tortellini. Place the finished pasta on a well-floured tray. Cover with plastic wrap and refrigerate until ready to use.

Bring a large pot of salted water to a boil. Cook the tortellini in the boiling water until al dente, with the filling heated through, 2 to 3 minutes. Drain well, and return to the cooking pot. Gently toss the tortellini with the Garlic Cream Sauce. Serve hot.

Pasta Medallions with Leeks, Ricotta, and Prosciutto

MEDAGLIONI DI PASTA CON PORRI, RICOTTA E PROSCIUTTO

Here is an unusual recipe, one full of explosive flavor. Family and friends will enjoy these medallions, and you'll enjoy the compliments that are sure to follow. You may wish to prepare this dish a day in advance, up to the final baking.

SERVES 4 TO 6

4 tablespoons olive oil, plus additional as needed

6 large cloves garlic, thickly sliced

¼ teaspoon red pepper flakes

2 cups thinly sliced leeks, white part only

6 ounces prosciutto or ham, chopped

¼ cup white wine

1 cup ricotta cheese

½ cup plus ⅔ cup freshly grated Parmesan cheese

1 whole egg

1 tablespoon chopped fresh Italian parsley

½ teaspoon salt

½ teaspoon freshly ground black pepper

1 recipe Fresh Pasta Sheets, Small Batch (page 40)

1 egg yolk mixed with 1 tablespoon water

1 cup Tomato Sauce (see page 229)

¼ cup thinly sliced fresh basil

Heat the oil in a skillet or sauté pan over medium-high heat. Stir in the garlic and red pepper flakes, and cook until the garlic is golden, about 1 minute. Add the leeks and reduce the heat to medium. Cook the leeks slowly, until they are tender but not brown, 4 to 6 minutes. Add the prosciutto or ham and wine, and simmer until the liquid is reduced to a glaze, 4 to 5 minutes. Remove from the heat and set aside to cool.

In a medium bowl, combine the ricotta, the ½ cup Parmesan, egg, parsley, salt, and pepper. Fold in the cooled leek-and-prosciutto mixture.

Trim three or four fresh pasta sheets to 14 inches long. Arrange on a piece of plastic wrap so they form a single large sheet roughly 10 x 14 inches. Let them overlap slightly; dampen lightly with the egg-yolk-and-water mixture where they overlap, and press to seal. Spread the ricotta mixture evenly over the pasta, leaving a 1-inch border on the narrower ends. With the aid of the plastic wrap, roll up the pasta into a thick log. Dampen the inch of uncovered pasta with the egg-yolk-and-water mixture, and press to seal the roll. Traditionally this is then rolled into a thin cotton cloth and the ends are tied with string to resemble a sausage. You may do this, or wrap the log completely in plastic and tie the ends in tight knots to seal them. Chill for at least 30 minutes for easier handling.

Bring a large, wide pot of salted water to a boil. (A fish poacher or deep roasting pan will work nicely if you do not have a pot wide enough to hold the roll.) Simmer the wrapped pasta roll for 35 to 40 minutes until the pasta is tender and the filling heated through. Carefully lift the roll from the water, let cool, and refrigerate until firm (at least 2 hours, preferably overnight). Remove the cloth or plastic and cut the pasta roll into 12 medallions, each about ¾ inch thick.

Preheat the oven to 450°. Lightly oil an ovenproof serving dish or 4 to 6 individual dishes, and arrange the medallions neatly, overlapping slightly. Drizzle with the Tomato Sauce, sprinkle with the remaining ⅔ cup Parmesan, and bake for 8 to 10 minutes, until brown. Remove from the oven, garnish with the basil, and serve.

Pasta Medallions with Wild Mushrooms and Truffle

MEDAGLIONI DI PASTA CON FUNGHI DI BOSCO E TARTUFO

This elegant rendition of pasta medallions is a sure hit with sophisticated palates, and even more so with those who have never experienced the particular combination of ingredients. You may wish to prepare the dish a day in advance, up to the final baking.

SERVES 4 TO 6

1 cup Chicken Stock (page 223)

½ ounce dried porcini mushrooms

5 to 6 tablespoons olive oil, plus additional as needed

½ pound white button mushrooms, sliced

½ pound cremini mushrooms, sliced

8 large cloves garlic, thickly sliced

½ cup white wine

1 cup heavy cream

½ teaspoon salt, plus additional to taste

¼ teaspoon freshly ground black pepper, plus additional to taste

1 cup ricotta cheese

½ cup freshly grated Parmesan cheese, plus additional for garnish

1 tablespoon chopped fresh Italian parsley, plus additional for garnish

1 egg

½ teaspoon truffle oil, or 1 small truffle, thinly sliced (see Chef's Tip)

1 recipe Fresh Pasta Sheets, Medium Batch (page 40)

Heat the stock to boiling and stir in the porcini. Remove the pan from the heat, cover, and let the porcini reconstitute for 20 to 30 minutes. Drain, reserving the stock. Coarsely chop the porcini.

Heat the oil in a large skillet over medium-high heat. Sauté the white and cremini mushrooms and garlic in the hot oil until they are browned and aromatic, about 2 to 3 minutes; cook the mushrooms in batches if necessary for a nice dark color. Add the porcini and wine, and stir to dislodge any browned bits from the bottom of the pan. Simmer until the liquid is reduced by half. Add the stock the porcini were soaked in, the cream, and the ½ teaspoon salt and ¼ teaspoon pepper, and reduce to a sauce consistency, 8 to 10 minutes.

Strain the sauce from the mushrooms, cover, and let cool, then refrigerate until ready to use. Combine the cooked mushrooms with the ricotta, Parmesan, parsley, egg, and truffle oil or truffle. Check the seasoning and add salt and pepper to taste.

Trim three or four fresh pasta sheets to 16 inches long. Arrange side by side on a piece of plastic wrap so they form a single large sheet of pasta, roughly 12 x 16 inches. Let them overlap slightly, lightly dampen where they overlap, and press to seal. Spread the mushroom–cheese mixture evenly over the pasta, leaving a 1-inch border on the narrower ends. With the aid of the plastic wrap, roll up the pasta into a thick log. Dampen the inch of uncovered pasta and press to seal the roll. Traditionally this is rolled into a thin cotton cloth and the ends are tied with string to resemble a sausage. You may do this, or wrap the log completely in plastic and tie the ends in tight knots to seal them.

Bring a large, wide pot of salted water to a boil. (A fish poacher or deep roasting pan will work nicely, if you do not have a pot wide enough to hold the roll.) Simmer the wrapped pasta roll for 30 to 35 minutes, until the pasta is tender and the filling heated through. Drain, let cool, and refrigerate until firm (at least 2 hours but preferably overnight). Remove the cloth or plastic and cut the roll into 12 equal medallions.

Preheat the oven to 450°. Lightly oil a serving dish and arrange the medallions, overlapping slightly, in the dish. Drizzle with half the mushroom sauce and sprinkle with additional Parmesan and parsley. Bake until lightly browned, 8 to 10 minutes. Serve hot, garnished with more Parmesan and parsley, and pass the remaining mushroom sauce in a gravy boat at the table.

Chef's Tip: *Because truffle oil is intense in flavor (and expensive), be careful to use only ½ teaspoon. If you can't find a fresh truffle, one from a can or jar will do.*

Pappardelle with Rustic Lamb Sauce

PAPPARDELLE AL RAGÙ DI AGNELLO ALLA RUSTICA

The term pappardelle *usually refers to wide-cut fresh noodles. This is my version of a recipe found, with some variations, throughout the Italian countryside.*

SERVES 4 TO 6

1 recipe Fresh Pasta Sheets, Small Batch
    (page 39)

Flour as needed

Freshly grated Parmesan cheese for garnish
    (optional)

1 recipe Rustic Lamb Sauce (page 228)

Dust the pasta sheets generously with flour and roll each up lengthwise. Cut into 1-inch-wide ribbons with a sharp knife. Unroll the pappardelle and toss with additional flour to prevent from sticking together. If you are not using the pasta immediately, hang it on a rack to dry.

Bring a large pot of salted water to a boil. Cook the pasta until just tender, 2 to 3 minutes. Drain well, and return to the cooking pot. Pour the Rustic Lamb Sauce over the pasta and toss gently over low heat for 1 to 2 minutes.

Serve hot, sprinkled with freshly grated Parmesan cheese if desired.

Passione

Pappardelle with Artichokes, Prosciutto, and Truffle

PAPPARDELLE DEL BARONE

Once upon a time only the very rich could afford dishes like this. Land barons throughout Italy were known to indulge in this delectable recipe, which I have adapted for more democratic enjoyment.

SERVES 4 TO 6

1 recipe Fresh Pasta Sheets, Small Batch (page 40)

Flour as needed

4 tablespoons olive oil

¼ cup finely chopped onion

4 large cloves garlic, thickly sliced

⅛ teaspoon red pepper flakes

4 ounces prosciutto or ham, thinly sliced and chopped

1 9-ounce box frozen artichoke hearts, thawed and diced, or 1 14-ounce can, drained, rinsed, and diced

½ cup white wine

1 cup Chicken Stock (page 223)

1 cup heavy cream

¼ teaspoon freshly ground black pepper

1 small truffle, thinly sliced, or ½ teaspoon truffle oil (see Chef's Tip)

½ cup freshly grated Parmesan cheese

2 tablespoons chopped fresh Italian parsley

Dust the pasta sheets generously with flour. Roll each up lengthwise, and with a sharp knife cut into 1-inch-wide ribbons. Unroll the pappardelle, toss with additional flour to prevent from sticking together, and set aside. If you are not using the pasta immediately, hang it on a rack to dry.

Heat the oil in a large skillet or sauté pan over medium-high heat. Cook the onion, garlic, and red pepper flakes in the hot oil until the onion is translucent, 3 to 4 minutes. Add the prosciutto or ham and artichokes, and cook until the artichokes brown, 8 to 10 minutes. Add the wine, stirring to dislodge any browned bits from the bottom of the pan, and simmer to reduce the liquid to a glaze, 1 to 2 minutes. Add the stock, cream, salt, and pepper. Bring to a boil, and simmer until the sauce

continued

has reduced and thickened, 10 to 12 minutes. Add the truffle if not using the truffle oil below, and cook 1 minute.

Bring a large pot of salted water to a boil. Cook the pappardelle in the boiling water until just tender, 2 to 3 minutes. Drain, and return to the cooking pot. Pour the sauce over the pasta and toss carefully, over low heat, with the Parmesan and parsley until the cheese has melted, 1 to 2 minutes. Turn the pasta out into a warmed bowl, drizzle with the truffle oil if not using the sliced truffle above, and serve.

Chef's Tip: *Make sure you use just one or the other—sliced truffle or truffle oil. A truffle from a can or jar, while not as spectacular as a fresh one, is perfectly appropriate for this simple dish. Because the oil is intense in flavor (and expensive), be careful to use only ½ teaspoon.*

Ravioli with Calabrian Sauce with Sausage

RAVIOLI CON SUGO DI SALSICCIA ALLA CALABRESE

This very earthy dish is emblematic of the cooking style of southern Italy.

SERVES 4 TO 6

4 ounces soppressatta or salami, minced

¾ cup ricotta cheese, drained of liquid

1 egg yolk

3 tablespoons freshly grated Romano cheese, plus additional for garnish

4 tablespoons freshly grated Parmesan cheese, plus additional for garnish

Salt and pepper to taste

1 recipe Fresh Pasta Sheets, Medium Batch (page 40)

Flour as needed

1 egg yolk mixed with 1 tablespoon water

1 recipe Calabrian Sauce with Sausage (page 242), heated

Prepare the filling: In a medium glass mixing bowl, combine the soppressatta or salami, ricotta, egg yolk, Romano, and Parmesan. Stir with a wooden spoon to combine well. Add salt and pepper to taste, stir, cover with plastic wrap, and set aside.

Line two cookie sheets with plastic wrap or clean kitchen towels dusted with flour. Divide the pasta dough into 4 equal portions; use one at a time. Sprinkle the remaining portions with flour, cover with plastic wrap, and set aside.

Lightly dust one sheet of the pasta and roll it through the machine according to the directions on page 39, starting at the thickest setting and progressing to the thinnest. About halfway through, cut the sheet in half to make it more manageable. Continue rolling each half-sheet to the thinnest setting.

Lay the two sheets on a lightly floured board. Each should be roughly 5 inches

continued

67

wide and 15 inches long. Trim the ends. With a ridged pastry cutter or a sharp knife, cut each sheet into 2½-inch squares, or as close as you can get to that with the dimensions of the sheet; you should be able to cut an equal number of squares from each sheet. Line the squares up in twos on the board.

Place 1 scant teaspoon of the filling in the center of half the pasta squares. Brush the edges of the filled squares and unfilled squares, one pair at a time, with the egg-yolk-and-water mixture. Place the unfilled squares on top of the filled ones, and press the wet edges together gently with your fingers to seal them. Lift the edges of the bottom pieces to meet the top ones if necessary. Remove the finished ravioli to the prepared cookie sheet, and continue with remaining squares. You should have a total of 12 to 14 ravioli for one pasta sheet; cover with a lightly dampened kitchen towel and set aside.

Proceed as above, rolling, cutting, and filling the remaining portions of pasta dough, until you have used all the filling. You should have 48 to 56 ravioli.

Bring a large pot of salted water to a boil. In small batches (depending on the size of the pot), place the ravioli in the boiling water. Do not overcrowd the pot. The ravioli will cook very quickly, in 2 to 4 minutes, first sinking, then floating to the top. The ravioli assembled first will need slightly more time than the last batch. Scoop the cooked ravioli out with a mesh strainer, drain *very* well, and place on a serving plate. Once all the ravioli are cooked and on the plate, spoon a small amount of hot Calabrian Sauce over them, sprinkle with grated Romano and Parmesan, and serve.

Chef's Tip: *To make tortelli instead of ravioli, cut the pasta into 2½-inch rounds with a cookie cutter. Fill, cook, and serve as you would the square ravioli.*

Pappardelle with Fontina and Asparagus Sauce

PAPPARDELLE CON SUGO DI FONTINA E ASPARAGI

A delectable cheese joins its favorite partner in culinary mischief.

SERVES 4 TO 6

1 recipe Fresh Pasta Sheets, Small Batch
    (page 40)

Flour as needed

1 recipe Fontina and Asparagus Sauce
    (page 247; see Chef's Tip here), heated

Dust the pasta sheets generously with flour. Roll up each lengthwise, and with a sharp knife cut into 1-inch-wide ribbons. Unroll the pappardelle, toss with additional flour to prevent from sticking together, and set aside. If you are not using the pasta immediately, hang it on a rack to dry.

Bring a large pot of salted water to a boil. Cook the pappardelle in the boiling water until just tender, 3 to 4 minutes, depending on the thickness of the pasta. Drain, and return to the cooking pot. Pour the hot Fontina and Asparagus Sauce over the pasta and toss carefully to coat well. Serve immediately.

Chef's Tip: *For a variation on this sauce and how to use it in this recipe: Follow the instructions on page 247 until you have whisked the egg yolks into the milk and soaked the mixture for 2 to 4 minutes. Pour the mixture over the cooked asparagus and keep warm over low heat. Cook the pasta as directed above, drain, and add the milk-and-asparagus mixture. Add the shredded cheeses called for in the sauce recipe and toss well. Serve immediately.*

$\mathscr{P}$umpkin Ravioli

RAVIOLI DI ZUCCA

You might surprise your guests with this traditional Italian dish at your next Thanksgiving dinner.

SERVES 4 TO 6

1 cup canned pumpkin purée

¼ cup heavy cream

¼ teaspoon salt

¼ teaspoon freshly ground black pepper

1 cup freshly grated Parmesan cheese

1 whole egg

1 recipe Fresh Pasta Sheets, Large Batch (page 39)

Flour as needed

1 egg yolk mixed with 1 tablespoon water

1 recipe Parma Sauce (page 240), heated

2 tablespoons chopped fresh sage

To make the filling, combine the pumpkin purée, cream, salt, and pepper in a small saucepan and cook over medium-high heat, stirring often, until the mixture is thick and pulls away from the side of the pan, 8 to 10 minutes. Remove from the heat, cool to room temperature, and stir in the Parmesan and egg. Set aside.

To make the ravioli, lay one sheet of pasta flat on a well-floured work surface. Place teaspoonfuls of the filling at 2-inch intervals on the sheet. The spoonfuls will each be individual ravioli, so make sure there is enough room between them to form and seal the pasta. Brush the egg-yolk-and-water mixture lightly around the dropped spoonfuls of filling. Place another sheet of pasta on top and press down gently with your fingers. Eliminate any air in the ravioli, or they may burst during cooking. Press more firmly to seal the layers, and cut the pasta with a wheel to make the desired ravioli shapes. Pull the pieces apart and dust generously with flour. Place the finished ravioli on a baking sheet or tray generously dusted with flour to prevent them from sticking together. Repeat the process with the remaining pasta sheets and filling. If you are not cooking the ravioli immediately, cover with plastic wrap and refrigerate until ready to use.

Bring a large pot of salted water to a boil. Cook the ravioli, in batches as necessary, in the boiling water until just tender and cooked through, 3 to 4 minutes. Drain well and divide among warmed plates. Drizzle with hot Parma Sauce, garnish with the sage, and serve.

Chef's Tip: *You might also garnish with toasted pine nuts or hazelnuts, or some freshly grated nutmeg. To toast the nuts, toss them in a little olive oil and bake on a nonstick baking sheet in a preheated 325° oven for 5 to 6 minutes, until they are a light golden brown.*

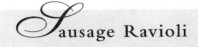

Sausage Ravioli

RAVIOLI DI SALSICCIA

In this version of ravioli, made with sausage and finished with a creamy mixture of ricotta and tomato sauce, a simple combination yields amazing flavor.

SERVES 4 TO 6

2 tablespoons olive oil

½ cup chopped onion

4 large cloves garlic, thickly sliced

½ pound spicy Italian-style sausage, casing removed, broken up

½ cup white wine

¾ cup ricotta cheese

¾ cup freshly grated Romano cheese

¼ cup Italian-Style Bread Crumbs (page 220)

1 whole egg

½ teaspoon freshly ground black pepper

1 recipe Fresh Pasta Sheets, Large Batch (page 39)

1 egg yolk mixed with 1 tablespoon water

Flour as needed

2 cups Tomato Sauce (page 229), warmed

2 tablespoons chopped fresh basil

To make the filling, heat the oil in a large sauté pan or skillet over medium heat. Add the onion and garlic, and sauté until tender, 4 to 5 minutes. Increase the heat to medium–high, add the sausage, and brown until it is cooked through, 5 to 6 minutes. Pour out all but 1 to 2 tablespoons of the fat in the pan. Add the wine, stirring to dislodge any browned bits from the bottom. Simmer until the liquid is reduced to a glaze, 2 to 3 minutes. In a food processor, combine the sausage mixture with ½ cup each of the ricotta and Romano, the bread crumbs, egg, and pepper, and process to a thick paste.

To make the ravioli, lay one sheet of pasta flat on a well-floured work surface. Drop teaspoonfuls of the filling onto the sheet at 2-inch intervals. The spoonfuls will each be individual ravioli, so make sure there is enough room between them to form and seal the pasta. Brush the egg-yolk-and-water mixture lightly around the dropped spoonfuls. Place a second pasta sheet on top and press down gently around the filling. Eliminate any excess air in the ravioli, or they may burst during cooking. Press more firmly to seal the layers, and cut the pasta with a wheel to make the desired ravioli shapes. Pull the pieces apart and dust generously with flour. Place the finished ravioli on a baking sheet or tray with flour to prevent sticking together. Repeat the process with the remaining pasta sheets and filling. Cover the finished ravioli with plastic wrap and refrigerate until ready to use.

Bring a large pot of salted water to a boil. In a small bowl, combine the remaining ricotta and Romano. Cook the ravioli, in batches as necessary, in the boiling water until just tender and cooked through, 2 to 3 minutes. Drain, and return to the cooking pot. Toss the ravioli with warm Tomato Sauce and the cheese mixture until well combined. Turn the pasta out into a warmed serving bowl or individual plates, garnish with the basil, and serve.

Scallop Tortellini with Pea Sauce and Prosciutto

TORTELLINI DI CAPESANTE CON SUGO DI PISELLI E PROSCIUTTO

This is a very elegant dish, with an intriguing interplay of flavors.

SERVES 4 TO 6

¾ pound bay scallops

1 tablespoon white wine

2 tablespoons heavy cream

1 tablespoon snipped fresh chives

1 whole egg

¼ teaspoon salt

¼ teaspoon freshly ground black pepper

1 recipe Fresh Pasta Sheets, Large Batch (page 39)

1 egg yolk mixed with 1 tablespoon water

Flour as needed

1 recipe Pea Sauce (page 249)

1 tablespoon olive oil

4 ounces prosciutto or ham, cut into thin strips

To make the filling, combine the scallops, wine, cream, and chives in a small bowl. Marinate for at least 10 minutes. Add the egg, salt, and pepper, and process in a blender or food processor to form a thick paste.

To make the tortellini, cut the pasta sheets into 2-inch squares. Place a teaspoon of filling in the center of each and fold it over into a triangle. Make a tight seal, dampening the edges lightly with the egg-yolk-and-water mixture if necessary. Pull the two ends of the longest side of the tri-angle around and pinch the tips together. Fold the remaining tip up to obtain the desired shape. Place the finished pasta on a well-floured tray. If you are not cooking immediately, cover with plastic wrap and refrigerate until ready to use.

Heat the oil in a skillet over medium-high heat. Fry the prosciutto or ham until crisp, 4 to 5 minutes. Drain on paper towels.

Bring a large pot of salted water to a boil. Warm the Pea Sauce gently over low heat. Cook the tortellini in the boiling water until just tender and cooked through, 3 to 4 minutes. Drain well, and return to the cooking pot. Add the Pea Sauce and toss gently over low heat to combine, 1 to 2 minutes. Spoon the tortellini onto a warmed serving platter and serve hot, topped with the prosciutto or ham.

$\mathcal{T}$agliatelle with Piedmontese Sauce

TAGLIATELLE AL SUGO PIEMONTESE

The version of this dish I had once in Turin was impressive, and I've tried to re-create it ever since. It is very rich, perfect for a cold winter evening.

SERVES 4 TO 6

1 recipe Fresh Pasta Sheets, Medium Batch (page 40), or 1 pound dry tagliatelle

Flour as needed

2 egg yolks

½ cup freshly grated Parmesan cheese, plus additional for garnish

1 recipe Piedmontese Sauce (page 239)

Generously dust the pasta sheets with flour. Roll up each lengthwise, and with a sharp knife cut into ½-inch slices. Unroll the tagliatelle and dust with flour to prevent sticking. If you are not using the pasta immediately, hang it on a rack to dry.

In a small bowl, whisk together the egg yolks and ½ cup Parmesan. Set aside.

Bring a large pot of salted water to a boil. Gently pat or shake the tagliatelle to remove any excess flour. Cook in the boiling water until just al dente, 1 to 2 minutes. If you are using dry pasta, cook it according to the package directions. Drain the pasta, and return to the cooking pot. Add warm Piedmontese Sauce and mix well. Add the egg-yolk-and-Parmesan mixture and toss to coat the pasta evenly. Cook over medium-low heat until the pasta and sauce are well combined and the egg has cooked through, 2 minutes. Serve in individual dishes with plenty of Parmesan sprinkled on top.

Timbale of Eggplant and Lasagna

TIMBALLO DI MELANZANE E LASAGNE

This excellent vegetarian dish will appeal to even the most ardent meat-and-potato fans at your dinner table.

SERVES 6

4 tablespoons olive oil, plus additional
    as needed

1 recipe Fresh Pasta Sheets, Medium Batch
    (page 40), or 1 pound dry lasagna

3 eggplants (3 pounds)

½ teaspoon salt, plus additional as needed

¼ cup Italian-Style Bread Crumbs (page 220)

¼ cup roasted garlic pulp (see Chef's Tip
    page 251)

¼ teaspoon red pepper flakes

½ teaspoon freshly ground black pepper, plus
    additional as needed

4 cups Tomato Sauce (see page 229)

¾ pound fresh mozzarella cheese, cut into
    ½-inch cubes (see Chef's Tip)

4 hard-boiled eggs, sliced

½ cup chopped fresh basil

Bring a large pot of salted water to a boil. Fill a large bowl with ice water mixed with a few tablespoons of oil. Cook 3 or 4 lasagna sheets at a time in the boiling water until al dente, about 1 minute. Lift the cooked sheets out and plunge them directly in the ice water. If you are using dry lasagna, cook the pasta according to the package directions. Drain and place the sheets flat on a lightly oiled baking sheet or tray. If you are stacking the sheets or storing for later use, brush or spray each with oil to prevent them from sticking. If you are not cooking immediately, cover the lasagna with plastic wrap until to ready to use.

Slice two of the eggplants into long, ¼-inch-thick pieces. Cut the third eggplant in half and score the flesh lightly with a knife. Sprinkle the cut surfaces of the eggplants with salt. Place them in a colander, cover with a small plate, and

continued

weight the plate with a heavy object for 10 to 15 minutes to extract the bitter juices from the eggplant. Pat the eggplant dry after doing so.

Preheat the oven to 500°. Brush or spray the eggplant slices with oil and place on two baking sheets. Roast for 18 to 20 minutes, flipping them once during cooking, until they are tender and brown on both sides. Remove the slices, reduce the heat to 450°, and place the halved eggplant, cut sides down, on a lightly oiled baking sheet. Roast until the halves are completely softened, 20 minutes. Cool slightly and scoop the flesh into a small bowl. Discard the skin.

Oil the inside of a deep rectangular baking pan and coat with 2 tablespoons of the bread crumbs. Line the bottom of the pan carefully with roasted eggplant slices, and arrange them also neatly around the sides, letting the longer slices flop over the edges of the pan. The bottom and sides of the baking dish should be completely covered with a tight series of slices.

Gently mix the roasted garlic pulp into the eggplant pulp. Season with the red pepper flakes and ½ teaspoon each salt and pepper.

Preheat the oven to 450°. Spread ½ cup of the Tomato Sauce on the eggplant at the bottom of the baking pan. Cover with a layer of the prepared lasagna sheets. Spread the pasta with ¼ cup of the eggplant-and-garlic mixture, and sprinkle with a quarter of the mozzarella, slices of 1 egg, and 1 tablespoon of the basil. Season with a pinch each of salt and pepper. Drizzle with ½ cup of the Tomato Sauce, cover with more lasagna, and repeat this layering to the top of the pan, finishing with a layer of pasta. Fold the eggplant slices flopping over the edges of the pan on top of the last layer. Sprinkle with the remaining bread crumbs.

Bake for 20 to 25 minutes, until the timbale is golden brown and bubbling. After letting the timbale rest for 10 minutes, carefully place a serving dish over the baking pan, invert the timbale onto the serving dish, and remove the baking pan. Serve cut into large pieces with remaining Tomato Sauce on the side.

Chef's Tip: *If the fresh mozzarella was packed in water, drain on paper towels before cutting into cubes.*

Tortellini with Smoked Salmon and Creamed Tomato-Caper Sauce

TORTELLINI AL SALMONE AFFUMICATO CON CREMA DI POMODORO E CAPPERI

This is my own creation, and I particularly like the encounter of flavors of the smoked fish and the sauce.

SERVES 4 TO 6

6 ounces smoked salmon or lox

6 ounces mascarpone or cream cheese

1 egg yolk

¼ cup heavy cream

2 tablespoons snipped fresh chives

¼ teaspoon freshly ground black pepper

1 recipe Fresh Pasta Sheets, Large Batch (page 39)

Flour as needed

1 recipe Creamed Tomato-Caper Sauce (page 232)

Make the filling: In a food processor, purée the salmon or lox, mascarpone or cream cheese, egg yolk, and cream. Season with chives and pepper.

To prepare the tortellini, cut the fresh pasta sheets into 2-inch squares. Place a teaspoon of the filling in the center of each square and fold it over to form a triangle. Make a tight seal, dampening the edges of the pasta lightly if necessary. Pull the corners of the longest side around and pinch together. Fold the remaining tip up to form the desired shape. Place the finished tortellini on a floured tray. If you are not cooking the tortellini immediately, cover with plastic wrap and refrigerate until ready to use.

Bring a large pot of salted water to a boil. Cook the tortellini in the boiling water until al dente and heated through, 2 to 3 minutes. Drain, and place on a large platter. Spoon the Creamed Tomato-Caper Sauce over the pasta and serve.

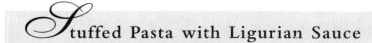

$\mathscr{S}$tuffed Pasta with Ligurian Sauce

PANSOTI CON SALSA LIGURE

I enjoyed a recipe similar to this while traveling along the Ligurian coast south of Genoa.

SERVES 4 TO 6

8 ounces mortadella or bologna, thinly sliced and chopped, plus 3 to 4 ounces cut into ¼-inch dice

½ cup pine nuts

2 large cloves garlic, chopped

½ cup ricotta cheese

¼ cup freshly grated Parmesan cheese, plus additional for garnish

1 whole egg

¼ teaspoon salt

¼ teaspoon freshly ground black pepper

1 recipe Fresh Pasta Sheets, Large Batch (page 39), or Fresh Spinach Pasta Sheets (page 41)

1 egg yolk mixed with 1 tablespoon water

1 tablespoon olive oil

1 recipe Ligurian Sauce (page 238)

1 cup diced fresh tomato

Make the filling: Combine the chopped mortadella or bologna, the pine nuts, and the garlic in the bowl of a food processor and chop to a coarse paste. Add the ricotta, ¼ cup Parmesan, egg, salt, and pepper, and purée. Transfer the purée to a bowl, cover, and refrigerate until ready to use.

Make the pansoti: Cut the pasta sheets into 2½-inch squares. Place a teaspoon of the filling in the center of each square, dab the sides with the egg-yolk-and-water mixture, and fold the square over into a triangle. Press out any air, and pinch the edges to seal the triangles. Place the pasta on a well-floured tray and dust with flour to prevent sticking. Cover with plastic wrap and refrigerate until ready to use.

Heat the oil in a large sauté pan or skillet over medium-high heat, add the diced mortadella or bologna, and sauté until crisp and brown, 2 to 3 minutes.

Bring a large pot of salted water to a boil. Cook the pasta in the boiling water until tender and heated through, 2 to 3 minutes. Drain, and place in a large bowl. Pour on the Ligurian Sauce and toss carefully to combine. Serve in individual dishes topped with the browned mortadella, diced tomato, and a generous dusting of Parmesan.

Chef's Tip: *It might be easier to find domestic bologna at your local store, but I urge you to look for Italian mortadella, which has only recently been approved for importation into this country. The search will be well worth your while.*

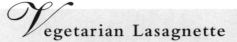

Vegetarian Lasagnette

LASAGNETTE DI VERDURA

This recipe proves conclusively that vegetables can make a meal fit for a king.

SERVES 6

4 tablespoons olive oil, plus additional
    as needed

6 large cloves garlic, thickly sliced

½ teaspoon red pepper flakes

1 cup chopped onion

1 cup diced carrot

2 cups diced zucchini

¼ cup chopped fresh basil

1 tablespoon chopped fresh sage,
    or ½ teaspoon dried

2 teaspoons chopped fresh rosemary,
    or 1 teaspoon dried

½ teaspoon dried thyme

½ cup white wine

½ cup chopped walnuts (optional)

1 cup Spicy Tomato Sauce (page 230) or
    Tomato Sauce (page 229)

½ teaspoon salt

½ teaspoon freshly ground black pepper

1 recipe Fresh Pasta Sheets, Small Batch
    (page 40), or 4 to 6 dry lasagna noodles

1 recipe Parmesan Béchamel Sauce
    (see Chef's Tips page 235)

⅓ cup freshly grated Parmesan cheese

Preheat the oven to 450°. Lightly grease 6 individual gratin dishes.

Heat the oil in a large skillet or sauté pan over medium-high heat. Add the garlic and red pepper flakes, and cook until the garlic is golden brown, about 1 minute. Add the onion and carrot, and cook over medium heat until the carrot is tender, 5 to 7 minutes. Stir in the zucchini and herbs, and cook over medium heat until the flavors are combined, 1 to 2 minutes. Add the wine, stir, and simmer until the liquid is reduced, about 2 minutes. Stir in the walnuts, if desired, and tomato sauce. Season with the salt and pepper, bring to a boil, reduce the heat to medium, and simmer until the vegetables are tender and the sauce is thick and glossy, 6 to 8 minutes. Set aside to cool.

Bring a large pot of salted water to a boil. Fill a large bowl with ice water mixed with a few tablespoons of oil. Cut the pasta sheets into pieces that will fit neatly into the gratin dishes (4-inch squares for similar-size round dishes; 3x5-inch rectangles for similar-size ovals). Cook the cut pasta a few pieces at a time in the boiling water until al dente, about 1 minute. Remove the pieces of cooked pasta and immediately plunge into the ice water. If you are using dry pasta, cook the whole pieces according to the package directions and then cut them as necessary after cooking and cooling. Drain the pasta well and lay flat on a baking sheet or tray. If you are stacking the sheets or storing for later use, brush or spray each piece with oil to prevent them from sticking together. Cover the pasta with plastic wrap until ready to use.

Place 2 tablespoons of the Parmesan Béchamel Sauce at the bottom of each gratin dish. Cover with a piece of pasta, top with 2 tablespoons of the vegetable-and-tomato sauce, and another tablespoon of the béchamel. Repeat with the remaining ingredients, finishing with a final layer of vegetables. Sprinkle each of the lasagnette with 1 tablespoon of Parmesan, and bake for 10 minutes, or until the tops are brown and bubbling. Remove the lasagnette from the oven and let rest for 3 to 5 minutes before serving.

"Accussì"

*I*n the summer of 1999, my wife, Nanci, and I traveled to Sicily to spend time with my parents at their apartment in Mondello, a seaside community not far from Palermo, where I was raised. One evening, as my father and I sat together on the terrace and enjoyed the beauty of the sun setting on the Mediterranean, I thought about the man next to me as he had been: family protector, unbeatable conqueror, fearless adventurer—at least in the eyes of a young boy. Today he seemed a contemplative sort, content to sit quietly and savor the fading day. I remembered another sunset, many years before, on the island of Ustica.

Ustica lies forty or so miles off the coast of Palermo. For a long time, city folks have retreated there for some well-deserved rest and relaxation. Many have built vacation homes on the island's rocky coast, and years ago the most intrepid among them chose locations on the side of the island where there was no electricity and the roads were all but impassable.

One summer, when I was about ten, my parents, my brother Mario, my aunt Buliti, and I spent a long weekend at one of Ustica's hotel resorts. On this occasion we invited my father's lawyer and friend Pino, whom my brother and I affectionately called Zio (uncle), along with his wife. On our first day there, Mario and I played on the beach and at the hotel pool while the adults devoted their time to their own leisurely pursuits. In the late afternoon, we all gathered near the pool for refreshment. Between sips of his drink, Zio Pino told us about a friend of his, a writer, who had built a villa on the island, at a place known as Faraglioni Assassini—Killer Rocks. This friend, Zio Pino continued, in a conspiratorial tone that should have warned us of an impending misadventure, had invited him to use the villa whenever he wanted. He pulled a set of keys extravagantly from his pants pocket and whispered loudly to my father, "Let's go have an adventure." (The keys, it turned out, were not for the house, which was never locked. They were for the writer's car, which had been left at the docks near the resort while he was in Palermo. He had dropped the keys off with Pino earlier that day.)

"The roads aren't too bad," Zio Pino went on, "and if we leave soon we can be there before sunset. Don Vincenzo, what do you say?"

My father hesitated for a moment and glanced at my mother, whose expression already betrayed her resignation to the inevitable follies of the two men.

"*Io non vengo,*" she stated bluntly. I'm not coming.

"*Neanch'io,*" agreed Pino's wife.

My father and Pino exchanged looks. "*Noi, invece, andiamo,*" they said, almost in unison: Well, we're going.

There are things in every man's life that are hard to explain, and I can't say what overcame me back then. I suppose that like most ten-year-old boys, I was simply reckless—leaping before I looked, speaking before I thought. So even though the hotel had everything I could want, I screamed out, "*Vengo anch'io!*"—I'm coming too! Before my mother could utter a word, my father grabbed my hand and de-

85

clared, "Nicolino's coming with us. We'll be back tomorrow by lunchtime." Then he told Zio Pino, "Let's meet in the lobby in fifteen minutes." As he dragged me along to our room, all I could do was wave a hasty good-bye to my mother, aunt, and brother, and Zio Pino's wife. Their stunned expressions were almost comical.

In the flurry of departure, I asked myself, What was I thinking? But I wasn't about to look cowardly in front of my father and his friend, so I gave my father a few things to put in a bag and we went to join Zio Pino in the lobby. After a rushed stop at a nearby market, we headed to the harbor to pick up the car.

As it happened, Zio Pino did not know exactly where this place was. We drove for what seemed hours, until the road ended. And there, at some distance, we saw the "villa"—a small, run-down white stucco house perched precariously above the sea.

The two men looked at each other as I cringed in the backseat. They lifted their shoulders, looked to the sky, and laughed aloud: *"All'avventura"*—Let's venture on!

With our few bags of provisions in hand we left the car and climbed a long flight of steps cut into the mountain. Once we reached the terrace of the house, the view was so spectacular that it banished any reservations I'd had about leaving the safety and luxury of our hotel. The sun was just starting to disappear below the horizon, and everything around us was suffused with an intense orange light. We stood together, staring at the sea, with only the sounds of our labored breathing and the crashing waves below us breaking the silence.

"Ueh, picciotti," Zio Pino said at last. "C'mon, boys. It's getting dark. Let's get going."

Once we were inside, a vain search for a light switch reminded us that this place had no electricity. My father felt around the kitchen cabinets for a flashlight, since in our haste we had not bought one in town. He emerged from under the sink proudly holding a stump of candle. Aided by its flickering glow, we continued the search for more light, for it was clear the stub wasn't going to last for long.

On the mantelpiece in the main room we collected a few clumps of wax, which we carried to the kitchen. As gloom enclosed the house, I thought of my mother and my brother, probably digging into big plates of steaming spaghetti in the hotel dining room at that moment.

With the kitchen lit, however tentatively, my father was ready to snap into action. He checked the propane stove to make sure we wouldn't be eating raw food, and with a triumphant flourish announced that the preparations could begin. He and Zio Pino enthusiastically started emptying grocery bags on the table.

"Where's the pasta?" My father asked Zio Pino, who was preoccupied in sorting out his own bag.

"What pasta?" he replied distractedly. "Where's the bread?"

They stared at each other, and then at me, with looks worthy of a Laurel and Hardy routine: Here's another fine mess you've gotten us into!

Zio Pino barely missed a beat. "Well, I've found the wine," he declared. "How about finding a couple of glasses." In Italy, there is no crisis too great that it can't be postponed for a fine bottle of wine. The two men drank slowly, and I waited anxiously, listening to the waves on the rocks and the growl in my stomach.

When my father finished the last drop of his wine, he approached the table with determination. He sorted out what provisions we did have, and rummaged through the cupboards to see whether there was anything there he might use. Garlic, tomatoes, milk, eggs, and a small piece of pancetta from our own shopping were already spread on the table, and to these he added some flour, olive oil, spices, and a few odds and ends that he'd found in the cupboards. He grabbed a knife from a drawer and set to chopping the garlic with a deftness that impressed me.

"But Don Vincenzo," Zio Pino said, "what are we going to do without pasta?"

"Check over there." My father pointed to one of the cupboards. "I think I saw some bread wrapped in a towel when I was looking for a flashlight."

Zio Pino reached in and emerged with the loaf—a nice big country bread. But his face betrayed his disappointment. He tapped on the loaf. It was hard as a rock.

"Don't worry," my father reassured him. Start cutting it up as well you can."

Meanwhile, I sat on a stool near my father, monitoring the candles. He seemed unconcerned as he chopped away attentively, the various ingredients arrayed before him. He obviously had a plan. He stopped his work and gathered the pieces of bread Zio Pino had cut, and put them into a big bowl with milk, an egg, some flour, and grated cheese. Then he resumed his own preparations.

At my father's instructions, Zio Pino put a big pot of water on the stove to boil, while my father tackled the soaking bread. He blended the mixture gently until it looked like a bowl full of dough. (This might turn into a meal, after all, I thought.) Then he plucked small pieces of dough from the bowl and made them into little finger shapes. Finally he approached the stove with a pan and a bottle of olive oil. Soon the air was filled with the familiar aroma of sizzling garlic, tomatoes, and spices. I was sent outside to set the table; we would be eating under the stars! As I lay the knives and forks out in the darkness, I could hear the men talking inside, bursting out in laughter. I hurried through my task and returned to the kitchen to the heady fragrance of the sauce now simmering in the pan.

My father dropped the bits of "pasta" into the boiling water and turned to Zio Pino and me. "Look at you two—*gli affamati*," he said. "Go sit down, my starving ones. It's almost ready."

A minute or so later, he exited the kitchen with steaming full bowls and set them before us with the finesse of a well-trained waiter. The tomato sauce glistened on what certainly resembled some sort of pasta. He grated cheese over each bowl and poured the wine. He even honored me with a half-glass, topped off with water. This had to be a special occasion.

Maybe it was because I was so hungry, but every bite of that dinner was delicious. We finished our abundant first servings and then ate more. I looked at my father with pride.

"Don Vincenzo, what do you call this creation of yours?" Zio Pino asked between big bites.

"*'Nca chissaccio. Accussì li fici!*" my father replied in his thick Sicilian. What do I know? I made them this way!

And so we christened this dish *accussì,* or "this way."

On that dark terrace, the waves crashing below us, the moon shining in the clear night sky, I sat close to my father, certain and content that he would always be my unbeatable conqueror and fearless adventurer. I was happy in the way only a child can be.

"Nicolino! Vincenzo! Come in for dinner!"

The sound of my mother's voice brought me abruptly back to the present, to the terrace at Mendello. As my father and I went inside the dining room, I laughed out loud. I turned to him and whispered, *"Accussì li fici."*

For a moment he looked perplexed, but then a big smile broke across his face. He too remembered that night in Ustica.

At the table, he and I told of our adventure. My mother tried not to laugh too much as she recalled that weekend, although I'm not sure whether she had known the whole story until this day. And my wife recognized, as clearly as this tale revealed my father's own impetuous nature, that her husband was indeed his father's son.

"Accussì li fici!" my father repeated. He turned to me and caressed the back of my head as he had when I was a child, and brought back again those memories from thirty years before.

Gnocchi

When I was a child, gnocchi was one of those
delicacies that my mother prepared as a special treat. It was also the
first dish she prepared with my wife when she and my father came
to visit us for the first time shortly after Nanci and I were married.
One day during that visit, my father and I went shopping for fresh
fish in the markets near the harbor. When we returned, I found our
small apartment filled with trays of the puffy little clouds of potato
mixture called gnocchi. They were laid out on the kitchen counter,
on the dining room table, and even on the bed. My mother and
Nanci had made enough gnocchi for an army. In retrospect, I think
my mother knew I would finish them all eventually. And so I did!

While I will declare without reservation that the way my
mother, and now my wife, make gnocchi is without compare, there
are as many valid variations in preparing gnocchi as there are cooks
in Italy. From the beginning, opinions differ as to what is right: Do
you boil the potatoes with the skins on or off? Or do you bake the
potatoes? As I am so often reminded in Italy, there are no rules,
there are only suggestions. And so it is with making gnocchi. And
all the suggestions are right, if they work for the cook.

Once the potatoes are cooked (see the recipe to check
whether I boil or bake), I find that using a handheld ricer
is the most effective way to mash the mash to the best

consistency. If the potatoes aren't cooked enough, though, they will offer resistance and may bend the handle of the ricer. Alternatively, you might use a classic hand-crank food mill, which is what my mother uses.

As with all fine things, making good gnocchi takes some patience. While mixing the dough you might despair that it will never reach a proper consistency. And the dough sticks uncomfortably to your fingers, at least during the first few minutes of shaping it. But don't panic. (If you become frustrated, stop what you're doing, treat yourself to a sip of wine, turn on some pleasant music, and then dive back into the mixing bowl to finish the job.) Eventually, even the most uncooperative dough will take shape and stop sticking to your fingers. And you will get that wonderful uniform consistency you were looking for.

A few words of caution:

- Depending on where you live, you may have to reduce or increase the amount of flour called for in the recipe, to compensate for the effects of humidity or altitude.
- Watch the flour! If you add too much, the gnocchi may turn out too chewy.
- Unless you like them a little heavier (and some people do), be careful not to overmix the ingredients.

The simplest way to form gnocchi is to roll the dough into strands about ½ inch to ¼ inches in diameter and then cut them into ½-inch or 1-inch pieces. You can shape the gnocchi also by rolling pieces of dough into 1-inch balls and pressing these gently with the tines of a fork, for a ridged pattern. Or you can roll the balls of dough along the tines of a fork, running your thumb down the back of the fork. The gnocchi will hug your thumb and will take on an interesting shape, with a dent in the middle (from your thumb) and ridges (from the fork tines) in the back. You can make a more decorative shape by pushing ½-inch pieces of dough lightly against the blade of a cheese grater with your thumb. This will give you the grater pattern on one side and the dent from your thumb on the other. In truth the shape doesn't matter as much as the handling: the less you handle the gnocchi, the less flour you will need.

As you'll see in the Chef's Tip to the basic recipe, you can make gnocchi ahead of time and freeze them. If you make more than you use at one meal, they make great leftovers. In fact, I think they might taste even better the next day. To reheat, sauté lightly sauced leftover gnocchi in a little olive oil.

Making gnocchi is somewhat like making bread, but a lot simpler. After one or two tries you'll get a feeling for the dough, and soon you'll be turning them out like a master.

nocchi

Here are a principal recipe and a variation. Read both and decide which you would prefer to try first. I like them both, and prepare one or the other as the mood strikes me.

The principal version should produce dumplings as light as air. But there is a trade-off. Light gnocchi are fragile. They will cook in boiling water in less than 3 minutes, so you will need to watch carefully that they do not overcook and fall apart. Since they are delicate, don't toss these gnocchi into the sauce; instead, pour the sauce on top before serving.

The variation, stronger and chewier, may cook a little longer and is better for reheating as leftovers.

SERVES 6

(MAKES ABOUT 100 GNOCCHI)

1¼ pounds baking potatoes, peeled and quartered (about 2 large)

¾ cup all-purpose flour, plus ¼ cup for dusting

½ teaspoon salt

¼ teaspoon freshly grated nutmeg

¾ cups freshly grated Parmesan cheese

Cover the potatoes with 2 to 3 inches of cold water in a large pot. Bring the water to a boil, reduce the heat, and cook over a low boil until the potatoes are easily pierced and broken apart with a fork, about 20 minutes. Drain well, and return to the pot on low heat for 1 minute to

dry. Remove the pot from the heat and let cool.

Combine the ¾ cup flour, the salt, nutmeg, and cheese in a bowl, and mix well. When the potatoes are cool enough to handle, press through a potato ricer into a large bowl. Add the flour mixture, pressing and kneading gently to combine. Turn the mixture onto a very lightly floured board; knead to combine the ingredients well, 1 to 2 minutes. Shape into a log, cover with plastic wrap, and refrigerate for 1 hour.

Remove the dough from the refrigerator and immediately cut it into 4 or 5 equal pieces. On a very lightly floured surface, roll and press each piece into a long, thin strand about ½ to ¾ inch thick. Pinch off pieces about ½ to 1 inch long (about ½ to 1 teaspoon of dough per piece). You may shape these pieces according to any of the methods described on pages 92–93. Place the gnocchi on a very lightly floured baking sheet or platter. Do not let them touch. Cover with plastic wrap and then a damp towel, and refrigerate until ready to use (within the same day; see Chef's Tip for freezing instructions).

Bring a large pot of salted water to a boil. Carefully place the gnocchi in batches in the boiling water, and cook for 2 to 3 minutes. They will initially fall to the bottom of the pot, but as they cook, they will rise to the surface. Remove with a mesh strainer or slotted spoon, and keep warm in a bowl covered with foil, which you might also place in a warm oven. Once all the gnocchi are done, serve with the sauce of your choice.

Chef's Tip: *Cook only the amount of fresh gnocchi that you will be eating immediately. You can freeze the rest: Arrange the uncooked gnocchi carefully on a baking sheet with space between them, cover well with plastic wrap, and place in the freezer. Once they are completely frozen you can remove them from the baking sheet to self-sealing plastic freezer bags. They will keep well for 2 to 3 weeks. To cook, drop the frozen gnocchi in boiling water and cook as directed above, for 3 to 5 minutes.*

Variation: *When I want my gnocchi a little chewier and stronger—so I can toss them into the sauce rather than the other way around—I rely on this method. It's also good if you know you'll be reheating leftovers. To the standard recipe add up to another ¾ cup flour, and 1 egg when mixing the flour and potatoes, and proceed according to the instructions above. As mentioned, you may have to cook these a little longer than the 2 to 3 minutes for the lighter variety.*

To reheat leftover gnocchi, sauté them, lightly sauced, in a little hot olive oil.

$\mathcal{B}$read Gnocchi with Tomato Sauce

ACCUSSÌ

This is my rendering of the dish my father improvised on Ustica when I was a boy.

SERVES 4 TO 6
(MAKES ABOUT 100 GNOCCHI)

3 packed cups cubed stale white bread, crusts removed

1½ cups whole milk

½ cup plus 5 to 6 tablespoons flour

½ teaspoon salt

¼ teaspoon freshly ground black pepper

1 large egg

⅜ cup freshly grated Romano cheese, plus 3 tablespoons for garnish

½ cup chopped fresh Italian parsley, plus 2 to 3 tablespoons for garnish

1 recipe Ustica Sauce (page 252)

In a medium bowl, soak the bread cubes in the milk for 10 minutes. Press down with a spoon to make sure all the cubes are submerged. Squeeze the bread to remove the excess milk, and transfer the bread to another medium bowl. Add ¼ cup of the flour, the salt, pepper, egg, the ⅜ cup Romano, and ½ cup parsley, and mix well. Add the 5 to 6 tablespoons flour, and mix well. The dough should be holding together well, but still a bit sticky.

Dust a board well with some of the remaining ¼ cup flour and turn the dough out onto it. Gently knead the dough into the flour on the board, adding more flour as needed. The amount will depend on how well the bread was squeezed; you probably will not use all of the flour. Add only enough to make a dough that will not stick when rolled. Less flour is better.

continued

Divide the dough into four equal parts. Roll one portion of the dough with your hands into ½-inch-thick ropes. Cut each rope into 1-inch pieces, and shape each of these into a small dumpling. Place the dumplings on baking sheets, not letting them touch, until ready to cook. Continue with the remainder of the dough.

Bring a large pot of salted water to a boil. When about ready to serve, drop the gnocchi in batches into the boiling water. They will sink first, and after about 1 minute will rise to the surface. Cook them for approximately 2 more minutes. Remove with a mesh strainer or slotted spoon, and keep the finished batches warm in a foil-covered bowl, which you might also place in a warm oven. Top the finished gnocchi with Ustica Sauce, Romano, and parsley, and serve.

Ricotta and Spinach Gnocchi

GNOCCHI DI RICOTTA E SPINACI

Another mouth-watering version of non-potato gnocchi, light as clouds and sumptuous in flavor.

SERVES 4 TO 6

¾ pound fresh spinach, stemmed and rinsed

1 scant cup ricotta cheese

1 large egg

¾ cup freshly grated Parmesan cheese, plus additional for the table

1 teaspoon salt

¼ teaspoon freshly ground black pepper

¼ teaspoon freshly grated nutmeg

¾ cup all-purpose flour, plus additional as needed

6 tablespoons unsalted butter

Cook the spinach in boiling water for 2 to 3 minutes, until completely wilted. Drain, and when it is cool enough to handle, squeeze dry. (It should be as dry as possible. After squeezing with your hands, wrap it in a clean kitchen towel and twist to remove even more moisture. The less moisture in the spinach, the less flour you will need, and the lighter the gnocchi will be.) Chop the spinach by pulsing in a food processor. Add the ricotta, egg, ½ cup of the Parmesan, the salt, pepper, and nutmeg, and pulse until completely combined. Transfer the mixture to a bowl, add the ¾ cup flour, and stir with a wooden spoon to combine.

Line two jelly roll pans or cookie sheets with waxed paper and sprinkle them with flour. Melt the butter in a large, deep sauté pan, and keep it warm over very low heat while you form the gnocchi.

continued

Generously flour your fingers. Spoon the spinach-ricotta mixture from the bowl by teaspoonfuls into your fingers, and gently shape and pat into oval dumplings. Place on the prepared jelly roll pans.

Bring a large pot of salted water to a boil. Drop the gnocchi by batches into the boiling water. They will sink first, then rise to the top as they cook. After they rise, cook them for 1 to 2 more minutes.

Remove with a mesh strainer or slotted spoon as they are done, and place in the pan with the melted butter. Increase the heat to medium-high, and toss gently in the butter. Sprinkle with ¼ cup of the Parmesan and toss. Serve immediately, with additional cheese passed at the table.

Chef's Tip: *For extra flavor, add 1 tablespoon chopped fresh basil or parsley to the spinach-and-ricotta mixture in the food processor.*

Gnocchi with Turkey and Bell Pepper Sauce

GNOCCHI CON PEPERONATA AL TACCHINO

SERVES 6

1 recipe Turkey and Bell Pepper Sauce
(page 241)

1 recipe Gnocchi (basic version, page 94)

6 to 12 tablespoons freshly grated Parmesan
cheese

Remove 1 to 2 cups of the Turkey and Bell Pepper Sauce to a gravy boat and keep warm. Turn the heat under the remaining sauce in the pan to low.

Bring a large pot of salted water to a boil. Add the gnocchi in batches to the boiling water. They will sink to the bottom first, then rise to the surface as they cook. Continue cooking for 1 minute after they rise. Remove with a mesh strainer or slotted spoon as they are done, and add to the sauce in the pan. Gently fold the sauce over the gnocchi.

Sprinkle each serving with 1 to 2 tablespoons Parmesan and pass the gravy boat with additional sauce on the side.

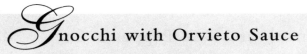

Gnocchi with Orvieto Sauce

GNOCCHI CON SUGO DI ORVIETO

This is ideal for restoring your energy and lifting your spirits on cold and dreary winter nights.

SERVES 6

1 recipe Orvieto Sauce (page 243)

1 recipe Gnocchi (basic version, page 94)

6 to 12 tablespoons freshly grated Parmesan cheese

Remove 1 to 2 cups of the Orvieto Sauce to a gravy boat and keep warm. Turn the heat under the sauce in the pan to low.

Bring a large pot of salted water to a boil. Place the gnocchi in batches in the boiling water. They will sink to the bottom of the pot first, then rise to the surface as they cook. Cook for 1 minute after they rise. Remove with a mesh strainer or slotted spoon as they are done and add them to the sauce in the pan. Gently fold the sauce over the gnocchi.

Sprinkle each serving with 1 to 2 tablespoons Parmesan and pass the gravy boat with additional sauce on the side.

Passione

Gnocchi with Arriminata Sauce

GNOCCHI CON SALSA ARRIMINATA

I love artichokes, and I've made it my mission to teach people how to pre-pare and enjoy them. This recipe will become a favorite of yours.

SERVES 6

1 recipe Arriminata Sauce (page 245)

1 recipe Gnocchi (basic version, page 94)

¼ cup freshly grated Romano cheese, plus additional for serving

Remove 1 to 2 cups of the Arriminata Sauce to a gravy boat and keep warm. Turn the heat under the sauce in the pan to low.

Bring a large pot of salted water to a boil. Add the gnocchi in batches to the boiling water. They will first sink to the bottom, then, within a minute or so, rise to the surface as they cook. Cook them for 1 minute after they rise. Remove them with a slotted spoon or mesh strainer as they are done, and add to the sauce in the pan. Gently fold the sauce over the gnocchi. Add the ¼ cup Romano and stir.

Serve with additional Romano and the sauce on the side.

Risotto

Risotto is a distinctive dish that seduces
your palate into culinary submission. Making it requires patience
and attention; a chef friend of mine once referred to the process as
a "tender caressing." Risotto is not a dish to be hurried, and in
these days of instant this and fast-food that, slowing down to prepare it can be an antidote to many cares.

To make a proper, traditional Italian-style risotto, I recommend Arborio, Carnaroli, Roma, Baldo, or Vialone rice varieties.
Italian chefs each have a favorite type of rice, usually depending on
their regional background; the most common in the United States
is Arborio. If you can't find any of the Italian varieties, you may
substitute domestic short-grain rice, although the flavor of the
risotto will not be quite the same. If you use a domestic short-
grain, you will need less liquid, usually between a third and a half
of the amount specified in the recipe. In addition, the cooking
time will be reduced by 5 to 10 minutes. The average cooking time
for a risotto dish is 25 to 35 minutes, varying according to the particular type of rice. The rice should be cooked until it is al dente,
or just tender to the bite but not crunchy. Classic risotto is smooth
and creamy, but there are two ways in which this consistency can
be achieved. As you might expect, both are the right way. Some
cooks prepare their risotto *all'onda,* roughly "like a wave,"

referring to the effect caused when you plunge a spoon into a big steaming bowl of this irresistible dish. Risotto *all'onda* is fairly loose and wet. Other cooks, however, prefer their risotto *asciutto,* or dry, with almost no extra liquid left in the rice.

In addition to the choice of risotto wet or dry, you have a choice of finishes. The cheese most commonly associated with risotto is Parmesan, although Fontina or Asiago is just as delicious and gives a creamier finish. You may add a splash of cream if you want things even richer. Then there is the *mantecatura,* the addition of butter at the final stage of preparation. If you choose to indulge in it, your risotto will have an extra sheen and an even richer taste.

Just when you think you've gone about as far off your diet as you can, here's a combination of finishes that makes this dish the ultimate culinary seduction: When the rice has finished cooking, turn off the heat, add butter, a little freshly grated Parmesan, ¼ to ½ cup heavy cream, and plenty of Fontina or Asiago. Let the risotto rest, covered, for 5 minutes, then very gently mix all the ingredients in the pan before serving. Don't bother counting calories if you choose to take this route.

For an extra special treat, or to give a flavor boost to risotto dishes, except those containing seafood or seafood sauce, add a dash of truffle oil just before serving. Truffle oil is usually olive oil in which pieces of truffle have been marinated. Because this infused oil is so intense in flavor, and expensive, you should use it sparingly. Half a teaspoon is sufficient in a risotto made to serve six people; any more than a teaspoon would overwhelm and ruin the dish.

Is there such a thing as risotto in a hurry? In spite of my earlier admonition, I'll let you in on a secret: If you're in the mood for risotto and your time is limited, there is a shortcut. Follow the basic recipe, but after adding the rice and deglazing the pan with the wine, pour in only half the amount of stock called for in the recipe; reserve the other half, and keep it very hot. Bring the liquid to a

boil, stirring, and then lower the heat, cover the pot tightly, and simmer the risotto for 12 to 15 minutes. Doing so eliminates the need to cook and stir for the first 15 minutes as called for in the traditional recipe. After that time, uncover the pot and add the remaining half of the stock, ½ cup at a time, as in the standard recipe.

You can also prepare the dish, up to the final additions of stock, in advance. You will need to add almost 2 cups more *boiling* stock than is called for in the standard recipe when you reheat the risotto. Add ½ cup at a time, stirring continuously until the stock is absorbed by the rice. This may not be exactly the same as the traditional risotto, savored immediately after its slow, careful cooking, but it is still delicious.

$\mathcal{R}$isotto with Pumpkin, Sausage, and Sage

RISOTTO CON ZUCCA, SALSICCIA E SALVIA

Pumpkin is a popular ingredient in the cuisine of northern Italy, and it adapts well to many different recipes. This one is perfect as is, but it can easily be turned into an equally flavorful vegetarian dish by omitting the sausage and substituting vegetable for chicken stock.

SERVES 4 TO 6

5 to 6 cups Chicken Stock (page 223)

1 15-ounce can pumpkin purée

4 tablespoons olive oil

1 pound sweet Italian-style sausage, casing removed

6 large cloves garlic, thickly sliced

¼ cup finely chopped onion

2 cups Arborio rice

2 tablespoons chopped fresh sage, or 2 teaspoons dried

½ teaspoon salt, plus additional to taste

½ teaspoon freshly ground black pepper, plus additional to taste

½ cup white wine

½ cup heavy cream

4 tablespoons freshly grated Parmesan cheese

In a medium saucepan, whisk together the stock and pumpkin purée. Bring the mixture to a boil, reduce the heat, and keep at a simmer.

In a large, heavy-bottomed pot, heat the oil over medium-high heat. Brown the sausage in the oil, breaking up the meat with a wooden spoon as it cooks, 6 to 8 minutes. Remove the pan from the heat, scoop out the meat with a slotted spoon, and set aside. Pour off all but 2 to 3 tablespoons of the fat in the pot.

Return the pot to the heat, add the garlic and onion, and cook over medium heat until the onion is tender, about 3 to 4 minutes. Stir in the rice, half the sage, and the ½ teaspoon each of the salt and pepper. Cook another minute, until the rice is well coated and slightly opaque. Return the meat to the pot and add the wine, stirring to dislodge any browned bits from to the bottom. Simmer until the liquid is reduced by half, about 1 to 2 minutes.

Add about 1 cup of the simmering stock-and-pumpkin mixture to the pot. Stir the rice constantly until the mixture is absorbed. Add another ½ cup of the stock mixture, and stir again until the liquid is absorbed. Continue adding liquid and stirring until the rice is just tender, about 30 minutes. Remove the rice from the heat and stir in the cream, Parmesan, and remaining sage. Check the seasoning and add salt and pepper to taste, and serve.

Chef's Tips: *If you prefer a looser risotto, stir in an additional ¾ cup stock after the rice has finished cooking.*

If you have any risotto left over, shape it into a log and refrigerate. Slice into cakes and fry them in olive oil until crisp, about 3 to 4 minutes per side. Serve the risotto cakes for a hearty brunch or a quick supper.

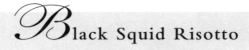

Black Squid Risotto

RISOTTO AL NERO DI SEPPIA

This dish is for the adventurous among you. The risotto will be dark brown, almost black—not your usual bowl of rice. But if you let yourself get past appearances, you will be delighted by its flavor.

SERVES 6 TO 8

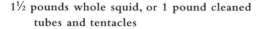

1½ pounds whole squid, or 1 pound cleaned tubes and tentacles

2½ cups clam juice

2 cups Chicken Stock (page 223)

1½ cups Tomato Sauce (page 229)

½ teaspoon squid ink (fresh from whole squid, or in small packets sold at fish shops)

4 tablespoons olive oil

1 cup finely chopped onion

¼ cup chopped fresh Italian parsley

6 large cloves garlic, thickly sliced

¼ teaspoon red pepper flakes

2 cups Aborio rice

½ teaspoon freshly ground black pepper, plus additional to taste

1 cup white wine

1 tablespoon finely grated lemon zest

Salt to taste

To clean the whole squid, rinse thoroughly and pull the tentacles from the body sacs. If you are using fresh squid ink, remove the slender silver ink sacs from the strands connected to the tentacles. Place in a small bowl covered with a few drops of water until ready to use. Clean the tentacles by cutting just below the eyes and retaining only the leg portion. Turn back the tentacles and squeeze gently to reveal the beadlike beak. Pinch off and discard. Gently squeeze the viscera from the tubes, making sure to remove the hard, transparent "quill" running the length of the interior wall. Peel the purplish skin from outside the tubes. Rinse the tubes and pat dry. Chop the tubes and cut the tentacles into quarters. Refrigerate until ready to use.

In a large saucepan, combine the clam juice, Chicken Stock, Tomato Sauce, and squid ink. Bring the mixture to a boil, reduce the heat, and keep at a simmer.

In a large, heavy-bottomed pot, heat the oil over medium heat. Add the onion, 2 tablespoons of the parsley, garlic, and red pepper flakes. Cook slowly, stirring often, until the onion is very soft but not brown, 8 to 10 minutes. Stir in the rice and squid, add the ½ teaspoon pepper, and cook until well coated and turning opaque, 1 to 2 minutes. Add the wine, stirring to dislodge any browned bits from the bottom of the pot. Simmer until the liquid is reduced by half, 1 minute.

Add 1 cup of the simmering broth to the rice-and-squid mixture. Stir the rice constantly, keeping the temperature at an even simmer, until the liquid is absorbed. Add another ½ cup broth and stir again until the liquid is absorbed. Continue adding broth and stirring until the rice and squid are just tender, about 30 minutes. Remove the risotto from the heat and stir in the lemon zest. Season to taste with salt and pepper. Sprinkle with the remaining parsley, and serve.

Chef's Tips: *For a richer taste, let the finished risotto rest for 3 minutes, and then fold in 4 tablespoons softened butter.*

If you prefer a slightly looser risotto, stir in an additional ¾ cup stock after the rice has finished cooking.

*R*isotto with Fennel, Pancetta, and Parmesan

RISOTTO ALLA PARMIGIANA

*This dish can be addictive. You think you can stop at just one serving?
Think again.*

SERVES 6

6 cups Beef Stock (page 221)

1 medium bulb fennel

1 tablespoon olive oil

1 pound pancetta, cut into ¼-inch dice, or
    bacon, cut into small pieces

6 cloves garlic, thickly sliced

½ cup finely chopped onion

¼ teaspoon red pepper flakes

2 cups Arborio rice

1 cup white wine

½ cup freshly grated Parmesan cheese

¼ cup heavy cream

Bring the Beef Stock to a low simmer.

Remove the stalks, fronds, and outer leaves from the fennel. Cut vertically (through the core) into quarters. Remove the triangular core pieces. Slice the quarters into ½-inch pieces. You should have 1½ to 2 cups fennel.

In a large deep sauté pan, heat the oil over medium-high heat. Add the pancetta or bacon and sauté until most of the fat is rendered and the pancetta or bacon is browned and well cooked, about 10 to 12 minutes. Remove with a slotted spoon and set aside.

In the same pan, sauté the garlic, onion, red pepper flakes, and fennel for 6 to 7 minutes, until the vegetables are softened. Add the rice and pancetta or bacon, and stir to coat the rice and combine the ingredients well, about 1 minute. Add the wine, scraping up any browned bits from the bottom of the pan. Stir well, and cook until most of the liquid is absorbed, 2 to 3 minutes.

Add the simmering stock 1 cup at a time, stirring frequently to keep the rice from sticking or burning, and allowing it to absorb the stock, about 2 to 3 minutes. Continue to add stock 1 cup at a time, until you have added 4 cups. Then add the liquid in smaller amounts, about ½ cup at a time, until the rice has finished cooking, about 30 minutes in all. (You may not use all the stock.) The risotto should now be creamy; it will "tighten" when served, so creamy is what you want.

Add ¼ cup of the Parmesan, about ¼ cup stock, and the cream, and stir to combine. Turn off the heat and cover the pot. Let the risotto rest for 2 minutes, then stir to combine the ingredients, and serve with the remaining Parmesan sprinkled on top.

Chef's Tips: *For a richer taste, allow the finished risotto to rest for 3 minutes, and then fold in 4 tablespoons softened butter.*

If you prefer a slightly looser risotto, stir in an additional ¾ cup stock after the rice has finished cooking.

$\mathcal{R}$isotto with Peas, Pancetta, and Mushrooms

RISOTTO CON PISELLI, PANCETTA E FUNGHI

It's magical what happens when you put together simple peas and mushrooms with pancetta. The combination conquers the palate as well as the heart.

SERVES 6

7 cups Chicken Stock (page 223)

¼ ounce dried porcini mushrooms, processed to a powder (about 2 tablespoons)

½ pound white button mushrooms, quartered

½ pound cremini mushrooms, quartered

3 tablespoons chopped fresh Italian parsley

1 tablespoon olive oil

1 pound pancetta, cut into ¼-inch dice, or bacon, cut into small pieces

6 cloves garlic, thickly sliced

1 cup finely chopped onion

2 cups Arborio rice

1 cup white wine

1 cup frozen peas

½ cup freshly grated Parmesan cheese

¼ cup heavy cream

Bring the Chicken Stock to a simmer. Combine the mushrooms and parsley in a bowl.

In a large, deep sauté pan, heat the oil over medium-high heat. Add the pancetta or bacon and sauté until most of the fat is rendered and the pancetta or bacon is browned and well cooked, about 10 to 15 minutes. Remove with a slotted spoon and set aside.

In the same pan, over medium heat, sauté the garlic and onion until softened, about 5 to 7 minutes. Add the mushroom mixture, stir to combine, and cook for 2 to 3 minutes. Add the rice and pancetta or bacon. Stir to coat the rice and combine the ingredients well, about 1 minute. Add the wine, scraping up any browned bits from the bottom of the pan. Stir and cook until most of the liquid is absorbed, about 2 to 3 minutes. Add the peas and stir to mix.

Add the simmering stock, 1 cup at a time, stirring frequently to keep the rice from sticking or burning and allowing it to absorb the stock before adding more, about 2 to 3 minutes. Continue to add stock, 1 cup at a time, until you have added 4 cups. Then add the liquid in smaller amounts, about ½ cup at a time, until the rice has finished cooking, about 30 minutes in all. (You may not use all the stock.) The risotto should now be creamy; it will "tighten" when served, so creamy is important.

Add ¼ cup of the Parmesan, about ¼ cup stock, and the cream. Stir to combine. Turn off the heat and cover the pot. Let the risotto rest for 2 minutes, then stir well to combine the ingredients, and serve with the remaining Parmesan sprinkled on top.

Risotto with Sausage, Radicchio, and Gorgonzola

RISOTTO ALLA PADOVANA

SERVES 6

6 cups Beef Stock (page 221)

1 tablespoon olive oil

¾ pound sweet Italian-style sausage, casing removed

½ teaspoon red pepper flakes

6 cloves garlic, thickly sliced

1 cup finely chopped onion

1 medium head radicchio, cored and outer leaves removed, and quartered and sliced into ¼-to-½-inch-wide ribbons

2 cups Arborio rice

1 cup white wine

6 ounces Gorgonzola cheese

¼ cup heavy cream

¼ cup freshly grated Parmesan cheese

Bring the Beef Stock to a low simmer.

In a large, deep sauté pan, heat the oil over medium-high heat. Add the sausage and cook until browned, about 10 minutes, breaking it into bite-size pieces with a wooden spoon. Remove with a slotted spoon and set aside.

Add the red pepper flakes, garlic, and onion to the pan, and sauté over medium heat until the onion is softened, about 6 to 7 minutes. Add the radicchio, stir to combine, and cook for 1 minute. Add the rice and sausage. Stir to coat the rice and combine the ingredients well, about 1 minute. Add the wine, scraping up any browned bits from the bottom of the pan. Stir and cook until most of the liquid is absorbed, 2 to 3 minutes.

Add 1 cup of the stock and approximately a quarter of the Gorgonzola. Stir to combine, then stir frequently to keep the rice from sticking or burning and to allow the cheese to melt evenly. Allow the rice to absorb most of the stock before adding the next cup, about 2 to 3 minutes. Continue adding 1 cup of stock at a time and a quarter of the Gorgonzola until you have added 4 cups stock and all the Gorgonzola. Add the stock in smaller amounts, about ½ cup at a time, until the rice has finished cooking, about 30 minutes in all. The risotto should now be creamy; it will "tighten" when served, so a fluid creaminess is desirable.

When the risotto is finished, add the cream and Parmesan, stir well, and serve.

Nicolino
e Mariolino

Not long ago, my wife and I were spending a quiet evening at home sipping a fine Amarone and looking through a box of old photographs. You might have a similar collection of pictures: unidentifiable snapshots, out-of-focus images, people in strange poses or with odd expressions—in other words, the photographs not quite good enough to put in your official album. Nanci and I love to sift through pictures like these. We always find some little treasure that reminds us of a story, a person, or a special place we had all but forgotten.

"What's this all about?" Nanci asked, holding a faded Polaroid. It was an image of my brother Mario and me standing next to our father's shiny new Alfa Romeo Giulietta. But it wasn't the two boys or the car that intrigued Nanci.

"What's with the beard and the mustache?" She pointed to a childlike scrawl across my face in the photograph.

That scribble I recognized right away: it was Mario's infamous signature. Every time we got into a fight, with Stealth-like precision he would locate photographs of me and add his artistry. In this case it was a big beard and mustache. I was older and bigger, so this was his way of getting the last word. This trick of his, which had angered me greatly as a boy, now brought a smile to my lips.

But there was something else captured in this photograph, something I had long forgotten. "Look at this. Look at his eyes, look at mine too." I pointed to our faces in the picture. "That, my dear Nanci, is the look of fear!"

It was the summer of 1968. We had left my grandmother's house in northern Italy and were returning home to Sicily. My mother was very close to her mother, and since Nonna Adele wasn't able to travel, we would go north to spend July and August with her.

My father always took advantage of this opportunity to show Mario and me different parts of the country. And so he would take different routes, depending on his mood: sometimes we would travel along the western, Tyrrhenian coast, while other times we took the central route across the Apennines. But it was the eastern, Adriatic coast, which was far less traveled and which afforded spectacular scenery, that was his favorite. I am sorry to say that my brother and I were not especially receptive to the natural beauty of these exotic locales. Those of you who have ventured on a road trip farther than your local mall with children in the backseat will understand the kind of stress we put on our parents. We were two rascals, always ready to get into trouble.

On that trip in 1968, my father had driven nonstop all the way from the Veneto to Puglia, the heel of the Italian boot. It was a hot day in August. The Giulietta did not have air-conditioning, and except for the open windows, which let in warm air, there was no way to escape the suffocating heat. My brother and I had been trapped in that car for many hours, and in spite of the beautiful vistas, the two of us had done nothing but fight. Both our parents were at their wits' end.

My father pulled off the freeway and followed a smaller coastal road. The shoreline was magnificent— long expanses of white beaches. There was no wind, and the sea lay almost flat. From the road you could see the sandy bottom under the turquoise water. That sight alone, finally, seemed to cool all our tempers.

Here and there along the road were remnants of once thriving fishing villages. In order to improve the southern economy, the government had allocated money for local communities to attract tourists. As a result, new family hotels had popped up on the shore.

At about five o'clock we stopped at one of these new hotels. Every room had an ocean view, we were told, and there was a pool—which, unfortunately, was empty—a full-service restaurant and a covered garage for the Giulietta. We checked in, had a pleasant dinner, and then went to bed.

Mario and I had our own room, separated from our parents' by a shared bathroom. The next morning, we two woke up at the crack of dawn. Our parents, exhausted from the long drive and our incessant bickering, were still sleeping. Mario and I were restless, and even though we had been given clear instructions not to leave our room until they had woken up, we decided to look around the hotel. And so, as quietly as we could, we left the room and made our way to the elevator.

It was dim inside, with only a single low-watt bulb working. Mario pushed one of the buttons on the panel. The door closed slowly, and the elevator began to descend.

When it stopped and the doors opened, we had no idea what floor we were on; whichever one it was, it was dark. The weak light from inside the elevator barely touched the pitch-black outside. My first instinct was to push another button and try another floor. But Mario was eager to do some exploring. Taking small, cautious steps, and with one hand extended in front of him, he stepped outside the elevator. Then, unexpectedly, he bumped into something big. "What's this?" He turned around to me. "Look, Nick, I think it's moving."

"Stop!" I whispered loudly. "Come back here!"

It was already too late. The dark undistinguished mass in front of us swayed slowly backward. We heard a crash, the sound of glass shattering. Now that our eyes had started to adjust, we could see the silhouettes of tall columns falling back against other columns. Two, three at a time, stacked cartons were toppling on one another. The whole place was shaking, and at our feet, first a rivulet and then a river of red was pouring into the elevator. I screamed, grabbing Mario, and he screamed as well. Then, suddenly, everything stopped. It was quiet again.

A light shone through the newly unobstructed window. I could see fallen cartons all around the floor and shattered bottles of mineral water, soft drinks, and wine. This time we were *really* in trouble!

We both jumped back into the elevator, and I repeatedly pushed the button to take us back to our floor. Once we got there, with the instinct of seasoned criminals, we pushed another button to send the elevator to another floor. This would cover our trail if anyone came to investigate the noise.

Mario and I ran to our room, where we sat petrified in our beds. It is the only time I can remember my brother and me able to face each other for so long without saying a word. It felt like an eternity had passed before our mother walked into the room. "Ready for breakfast?" she asked. We both shook our heads. "All right," she said. "I know, you want to get going. We'll grab something on the road."

The porter came to help us with our luggage, and my father stopped at the front desk to pay the bill. Mario and I were alert and ready for whatever might happen. I could hear my heart beating, and could hardly speak. Mario kept quiet too. Once the bags were loaded in the car, we breathed a sigh of relief. We just wanted to get in the car and get out of there.

Before we could leave, though, my mother turned to my father and asked,

"Why don't we get a picture of the boys standing by the car?" He agreed, and we posed—reluctantly—by the Giulietta. Just as he was taking the picture, Mario and I saw the manager exit the hotel, calling out and gesticulating wildly. So what the camera captured at that moment was the expression of pure, unadulterated fear. The gig was up; we were busted.

The manager ran over to us. "Mr. Stellino," he said to my father, "your wallet, you forgot your wallet." And then we heard shouting from the hotel lobby.

The porter who had carried our bags came out yelling. "The basement, the bottles . . . everything's destroyed . . . It's all a mess!"

The manager excused himself and went back inside. Without a word, we got into the car, my father started the engine, and we drove away.

During the entire trip home, Mario and I were silent in the backseat, and my mother complimented us on our gentlemanly behavior. She never found out what happened . . . until now, that is. I wonder what she will say when she reads this story. And as for Mariolino and Nicolino, that was the last of our exploring—for a while!

Pizza

I might be in my forties, but I love pizza as much as I did when I was a child. I have enjoyed every variation I've tasted, from the usual thick- or thin-crust varieties to the less ordinary stuffed versions.

For many Americans, pizza was their first introduction to Italian food, or what passed for it, if you don't count spaghetti in a can. At one time it was rumored that pizza, so common in the United States, was not even known in Italy—a story swallowed by those who have never been to Naples, where pizza originated and whose emigrants were responsible for spreading the pleasures of pizza throughout Italy and the world. I am sure generations of Neapolitans would be amused by the story. Well, perhaps there are American variations that you won't find anywhere in Italy, including the American-Style Pepperoni Pizza in this book.

As with all food traditions, pizza has been transformed over the years to reflect regional tastes and preferences. Sicilian-style pizza is traditionally baked in a deep dish or pizza pan, where it forms a thicker crust. I prefer the Sicilian dough, especially for stuffed pizza, pizza dumplings, and calzones.

Many people would argue that to make the perfect pizza, you must have a wood-burning stove. Since most of us do not have one in our home kitchens, I recommend using a pizza stone, which allows for an even heat under the dough, to bake the crust evenly. You might also want to get the long-handled, wide, wooden spatula known as a pizza peel. It is used to place the pizza on the stone, which is preheated in the oven, and to retrieve it without burning your hands.

Most home ovens may accommodate only a single pizza at a time if the pizza is to bake evenly in the middle of the oven. Since many of the recipes are for two pizzas, if you have a smaller oven, I suggest you assemble both, bake one, and cover the other with plastic wrap and refrigerate until ready to bake.

In most of the recipes following, I recommend using a moderate amount of sauce and toppings so as not to overwhelm the crust. Pizza is a versatile dish, and a personal one, so you can experiment to your heart's delight.

While I encourage you to make pizza dough from scratch, you can use many of the sauce recipes here with good-quality prebaked pizza dough. Keep in mind, though, that it will take less time for the pizza to cook; follow any package directions regarding handling and baking time.

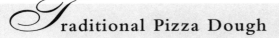

Traditional Pizza Dough

IMPASTO PER LA PIZZA

Here is a basic recipe for all your pizza needs, which you will enjoy time and time again. Takeout might even become a distant memory.

MAKES DOUGH FOR 2 14-INCH PIZZAS

1½ cups warm water

¾ tablespoon dry yeast (1 ¼-ounce package)

1 teaspoon sugar

4 cups all-purpose flour

1 teaspoon salt

3 tablespoons olive oil, plus additional
    as needed

Stir together the water, yeast, and sugar. Let the mixture rest until the yeast blooms, 3 to 4 minutes.

Place 3 cups of the flour and the salt in a mixing bowl. Add the yeast mixture and oil, and stir together to form a sticky dough. Knead, adding the remaining flour a little at a time, until the dough becomes a smooth, elastic ball, about 5 to 8 minutes. If you prefer to use an electric mixer, combine the ingredients with the paddle attachment and then change to the dough hook. Add the flour, a little at a time, until the dough is smooth and comes away from the sides of the bowl, about 2 to 4 minutes.

Turn the dough into a lightly oiled bowl and cover with a dry cloth or plastic wrap. Let rise for 30 minutes in a draft-free spot before stretching or rolling into the desired shape.

Chef's Tip: *Pizza dough does not require as much kneading or rising time as many bread doughs. If you are in a hurry, knead only until it forms a smooth ball. If you have the time, though, knead it further to strengthen the gluten. The result will be a chewy, stronger crust.*

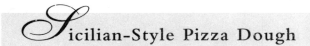

Sicilian-Style Pizza Dough

IMPASTO ALLA SICILIANA

1½ cups warm water

1½ tablespoons dry yeast (2 ¼-ounce packages)

1 teaspoon sugar

4 cups all-purpose flour

1½ teaspoons salt

1 tablespoon olive oil, plus additional as needed

Stir together the water, yeast, and sugar. Let the mixture rest until the yeast blooms, about 5 minutes.

Place 3 cups of the flour and the salt in a mixing bowl. Add the yeast mixture and 1 tablespoon oil, and stir together to form a sticky dough. Knead, adding the remaining flour a little at a time, until the dough becomes a smooth, elastic ball, 5 to 8 minutes. If you prefer to use an electric mixer, combine the ingredients with the paddle attachment and then change to the dough hook. Add the flour, a little at a time, until the dough is smooth and comes away from the sides of the bowl, about 2 to 4 minutes.

Turn the dough into a lightly oiled bowl and cover with a dry cloth or plastic wrap. Let rise for 30 minutes in a draft-free spot to double in bulk before shaping and filling.

Passione

Pizza Palermo Style

SFINCIONELLO

I used to sneak out of school early to be first in line to buy a slice of this from the vending cart that came around each day. Of all the recipes here, this one reminds me most of my boyhood.

SERVES 4 TO 6

3 large onions, thickly sliced

1½ cups Beef Stock (page 221) or Chicken Stock (page 223)

½ cup dry Marsala or port wine

1 bay leaf

½ teaspoon dried thyme

¼ teaspoon salt

¼ teaspoon freshly ground black pepper

2 tablespoons olive oil

1 recipe Sicilian-Style Pizza Dough (page 128)

4 ounces Romano cheese, half cut into ¼-inch dice, half finely grated

½ cup Pizza Sauce (page 233)

2 tablespoons Italian-Style Bread Crumbs (page 220)

Combine the onions, stock, Marsala or port, bay leaf, thyme, salt, and pepper in a large, heavy pot. Bring the mixture to a boil, reduce the heat to medium-low, and simmer, uncovered, for about 45 minutes, stirring often to prevent sticking or burning. The finished onions will be dark and sweet, and most of the liquid will evaporate. Remove the pot from the heat and cool the mixture to room temperature.

Preheat the oven to 500°. Grease a rectangular baking sheet generously with the oil. Roll or stretch the pizza dough onto the sheet and sprinkle evenly with the diced Romano. Press the cheese gently into the dough. Brush the surface with the Pizza Sauce. Top with an even layer of the onion mixture, and sprinkle that with the grated Romano and bread crumbs.

Let the pizza rise for 15 to 20 minutes in a draft-free spot. Bake for 15 to 20 minutes in the middle of the oven, rotating it 180 degrees halfway through the baking. When done, it will be nicely browned and bubbling. Slice into rectangles, and serve hot.

PIZZA

Baked Calzones with Prosciutto and Mozzarella

CALZONI AL FORNO CON PROSCIUTTO E MOZZARELLA

Here is a shining example of a recipe in the Sicilian tradition. These are easy to make ahead and reheat the next day. Kids love them.

MAKES 16 4-TO-5-INCH CALZONES

¾ pound fresh mozzarella cheese

1 recipe Sicilian-Style Pizza Dough (page 128)

8 ounces prosciutto or ham, cut into 16 thin slices

Flour or cornmeal for dusting

1 egg yolk mixed with 1 tablespoon water

Slice the mozzarella into 16 thick slices, and if the cheese was packed in water, drain well on paper towels.

Preheat the oven to 450°.

Divide the pizza dough equally into 16 balls. Roll each into a 4-to-5-inch round. Roll a slice of prosciutto or ham around a slice of mozzarella and place it in the middle of the dough. Fold the dough over the filling to form a half-moon, and press or pinch to seal the edges. Place the formed calzones on a baking sheet or pizza pan well dusted with flour or cornmeal. Cover with a dry cloth and let rise in a draft-free spot for 20 to 30 minutes.

Bake in the middle of the oven until the dough is golden brown, 12 to 15 minutes. Brush lightly with the egg-yolk-and-water mixture, and return to the oven to glaze, 1 minute more. Serve hot or warm.

Four-Cheese Pizza

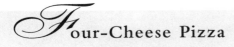

PIZZA AI QUATTRO FORMAGGI

While I am a strong believer in the saying "Less is more," I also believe in the concept "The more the merrier," and here is proof of that.

MAKES 2 14-INCH PIZZAS

½ cup freshly grated mozzarella cheese
½ cup freshly grated Parmesan cheese
¼ cup freshly grated Asiago cheese
¼ cup crumbled Gorgonzola cheese
1 recipe Traditional Pizza Dough (page 127)
Flour or cornmeal for dusting
½ cup Pizza Sauce (page 233)

Combine the four cheeses in a bowl.

Preheat the oven to 500°. If you are using a pizza stone, place it on a middle rack and preheat it with the oven. If you are using pizza pans, arrange the rack in the middle of the oven.

Divide the pizza dough in half. Pat or roll each half into a 14-inch round. Place on a wooden pizza peel or a pizza pan generously dusted with flour or cornmeal. Spread half the Pizza Sauce evenly over each round and distribute half the mixed cheeses over the sauce on each. Cover the pizza you will not be baking immediately with plastic wrap and refrigerate.

If you are using a pizza stone, slide the pizza directly onto the preheated stone. Otherwise, place the prepared pizza on its pan on the rack. Bake for 8 to 10 minutes, until brown, crisp, and bubbling. Remove from the oven, cut into wedges, and serve. Bake the second pizza similarly.

PIZZA

Baked Pizza Rolls with Sausage and Ricotta

ROLLINI AL FORNO CON SALSICCIA E RICOTTA

*Now we are entering deeper into my territory. When I was a kid I must
have spent all my weekly allowances buying these delicious rolls from a
shop near my school. My mother always worried that I wouldn't eat lunch
at home, but trust me, that was never a problem.*

MAKES 16 6-TO-7-INCH ROLLS

1 tablespoon olive oil, plus additional
    as needed

1 pound spicy Italian-style sausage, casing
    removed

1 cup ricotta cheese

1 cup freshly grated Romano cheese

1 whole egg

¼ teaspoon salt

½ teaspoon freshly ground black pepper

1 recipe Sicilian-Style Pizza Dough (page 128)

Flour or cornmeal for dusting

1 egg yolk mixed with 1 tablespoon water

Heat the 1 tablespoon oil in a large skillet
over medium-high heat. Add the sausage
and cook, breaking it up with a wooden
spoon, until it is browned and cooked
through, 5 to 6 minutes. The sausage
should be finely crumbled; if it is not,
chop it with a knife. Drain on paper towels, and set aside to cool.

In a medium bowl, stir together the
ricotta, Romano, egg, salt, and pepper.

Preheat the oven to 475°. Divide the
raised dough equally into 16 balls. On a
lightly oiled surface, roll or pat the balls
into 4x6-inch rectangles. Spread 1 tablespoon of the cheese mixture evenly over
each rectangle and sprinkle with a heaping
tablespoon of the sausage. Roll the rectangles into cigar shapes. Place seam side
down on a baking sheet dusted with flour

or cornmeal. Cover with a dry cloth and let rise in a draft-free spot for 15 to 20 minutes.

Bake in the middle of the oven for 8 to 10 minutes, until the tops are dark brown. Remove from the oven, brush lightly with the egg-yolk-and-water mixture, and return to the oven to glaze for 1 minute. Let cool slightly, and serve warm.

Chef's Tip: *These rolls are good on their own, but they're also excellent served with a dipping sauce such as Spicy Tomato Sauce (page 230).*

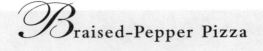 

Braised-Pepper Pizza

PIZZA ALLA PEPERONATA

*The sweet and sultry taste of cooked peppers will leave your guests begging
for more.*

MAKES 2 14-INCH PIZZAS

⅓ cup olive oil

1 medium onion, sliced

2 red and 2 yellow bell peppers, seeded and
    sliced

6 large cloves garlic, thickly sliced

½ teaspoon red pepper flakes

½ teaspoon salt

½ teaspoon freshly ground black pepper

1 recipe Traditional Pizza Dough (page 127)

Flour or cornmeal for dusting

½ cup Pizza Sauce (page 233)

1 cup freshly grated provolone cheese

½ cup freshly grated mozzarella cheese

Heat the oil in a large skillet over
medium-high heat. Add the onion and
cook, stirring, until it begins to brown,
2 minutes. Add the bell peppers and sauté
until they begin to brown, 4 minutes. Add
the garlic, red pepper flakes, salt, and black
pepper. Reduce the heat to low, and cook,
stirring occasionally, until the bell peppers
are tender, 20 minutes. The peppers and
onion will be dark, soft, and caramelized.

Preheat the oven to 500°. If you are using
a pizza stone, place it on a middle rack and
preheat it with the oven. If you are using a
pizza pan, arrange the rack in the middle
of the oven.

Divide the pizza dough in half. Pat or roll
each half into a 14-inch round. Place on a
wooden pizza peel or a pizza pan generously dusted with flour or cornmeal.
Spread half the Pizza Sauce evenly over
each round. Distribute half the bell pepper
mixture over the sauce on each, and top

Passione

with half of each cheese. Cover the pizza you will not be baking immediately with plastic wrap and refrigerate.

If you are using a pizza stone, slide the pizza directly onto the preheated stone. Otherwise, place the prepared pizza on its pan on the rack. Bake for 8 to 10 minutes, until brown, crisp, and bubbling. Remove from the oven, cut into wedges, and serve. Bake the second pizza similarly.

Chickpea Pizza Lucca Style

PIZZA CECINA ALLA LUCCHESE

Every time I make this at home, I remember sitting at an outdoor restaurant in Lucca, trying to persuade my wife to take a bit of what was to her a strange pizza. She did—and then she finished the whole thing.

SERVES 4 TO 6

Olive oil as needed

3 cups cold water

2 cups chickpea flour (available at specialty shops and health food stores)

1 teaspoon salt, plus additional to taste

½ teaspoon freshly ground black pepper

2 tablespoons chopped fresh basil

6 tablespoons freshly grated Parmesan cheese

Lightly oil a 12-inch nonstick pizza pan. Preheat the oven to 500°. Place the rack in the middle of the oven.

In a medium saucepan, stir together the water, chickpea flour, 1 teaspoon salt, and pepper. Bring the mixture to a boil over medium-high heat, stirring regularly to prevent lumps from forming. The mixture will gradually thicken. Cook until it starts pulling away from the sides of the pan and a wooden spoon can stand up straight by itself in the middle, about 20 minutes.

Remove the pan from the heat and mix in the basil and Parmesan. Pour the mixture onto the prepared pizza pan and spread in a thin, even layer. Let cool to room temperature.

Bake the pizza until brown and crisp, about 15 to 20 minutes. Sprinkle with salt as desired, and drizzle with your best olive oil. Cut into squares and serve warm.

Pizza with Caramelized Onion, Roasted Garlic,
Prosciutto, and Gorgonzola

Gnocchi with Arriminata Sauce

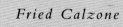 *Fried Calzone*

Risotto with Pumpkin, Sausage, and Sage

Creamy Fennel and Prosciutto Pizza

PIZZA MATTA

Matta means "crazy," and you won't find this madcap pizza anywhere in Italy; I created it by using what I found in the refrigerator. Sometimes the best ideas come when you least expect them.

MAKES 2 14-INCH PIZZAS

1 pound fresh fennel bulb, thinly sliced

½ cup heavy cream

½ cup Chicken Stock (page 223)

¼ teaspoon salt

1 recipe Traditional Pizza Dough (page 127)

Flour or cornmeal for dusting

4 ounces prosciutto or ham, thinly sliced and cut into ribbons

1 cup freshly grated Fontina cheese

½ cup freshly grated Parmesan cheese

½ teaspoon freshly ground black pepper

2 tablespoons chopped fresh Italian parsley

In a medium saucepan, mix the fennel, cream, stock, and salt, and bring to a boil. Reduce the heat and simmer until the fennel is tender, 30 minutes. Remove the fennel with a slotted spoon and boil the cream mixture until it is reduced to about ¼ cup, 4 to 5 minutes.

Preheat the oven to 500°. If you are using a pizza stone, place it on a middle rack and preheat it with the oven. If you are using a pizza pan, arrange the rack in the middle of the oven.

Divide the pizza dough in half. Pat or roll each half into a 14-inch round. Place on a wooden pizza peel or a pizza pan generously dusted with flour or cornmeal. Spread each round evenly with half the reduced cream mixture. Distribute each with half the fennel and half the prosciutto or ham, and sprinkle with half the

continued

cheeses and half the pepper. Cover the pizza you will not be baking immediately with plastic wrap and refrigerate.

If you are using a pizza stone, slide the pizza directly onto the preheated stone. Otherwise, place the prepared pizza on its pan on the rack. Bake for 8 to 10 minutes, until brown, crisp, and bubbling. Remove from the oven, cut into wedges, and serve. Bake the second pizza similarly.

Fried Calzones

CALZONI FRITTI ALLA SFIZIOSA

When I was a little boy, my mother, worried that I was overweight, took me to a doctor. He put me on a diet, and I followed it religiously—at home. On the way to school and back, though, I stopped at my favorite shop for a fill-up of these delicious calzones. My mother was so disappointed with the results of the diet that she let me abandon it.

MAKES 16 4-TO-5-INCH CALZONES

1 recipe Basil Parmesan Béchamel Sauce (see Chef's Tips page 235)

1 pound prosciutto or ham, chopped

8 ounces Gruyère or other good-quality Swiss cheese, shredded

1 egg

¼ teaspoon freshly ground black pepper

1 recipe Sicilian-Style Pizza Dough (page 128)

Olive oil for greasing

Flour for dusting

Extralight olive oil for deep-frying

In a medium bowl, stir together the béchamel sauce, prosciutto or ham, cheese, egg, and pepper.

When the pizza dough has risen, divide it equally into 16 balls. On a lightly oiled work surface, flatten a ball of dough into a 5-inch round. Place ¼ cup of the béchamel mixture in the middle of the round. Fold the dough over to make a half-moon, and press or crimp the edges tightly to seal them. Place the formed calzone on a lightly floured cookie sheet or pizza pan. Repeat these steps with the remaining dough and filling. Let the calzones rise, covered with a dry cloth in a draft-free spot, for 15 minutes.

Fill a wok or deep-fryer with at least 4 inches of the extralight oil, and heat to 375°. Fry the calzones, 3 or 4 at a time, until puffy and golden brown, about 1½ minutes per side. Drain on paper towels, and serve hot or warm.

continued

PIZZA

Chef's Tip: *To bake rather than fry the calzones, preheat the oven to 500°. Bake in the middle of the oven on a baking sheet or pizza pan for 12 to 14 minutes, until the crust is brown and the filling heated through.*

Fried Pizza Dumplings Stuffed with Meat Sauce

RAVAZZATE FRITTE AL SUGO DI CARNE

I think I first fell in love with this dish because I could not pronounce its name and my father had to order it for me. I did know how to point, however, and in good time I learned how to order properly. Meanwhile, I never went hungry.

You may make the sauce a day ahead, and refrigerate it overnight.

MAKES 24 3-INCH DUMPLINGS

4 tablespoons olive oil

1 stalk celery, chopped

1 medium carrot, chopped

½ cup diced onion

4 cloves garlic, thickly sliced

2 tablespoons chopped fresh basil

1 tablespoon chopped fresh Italian parsley

2 teaspoons chopped fresh sage, or 1 teaspoon dried

1 bay leaf

¼ teaspoon red pepper flakes

½ pound ground beef, lamb, or veal

2 ounces prosciutto or ham, chopped

¼ cup red wine

1 cup Tomato Sauce (page 229)

2 tablespoons tomato paste

½ cup Beef Stock (page 221) or Chicken Stock (page 223)

1 teaspoon salt

½ teaspoon freshly ground black pepper

1 cup frozen peas, thawed

1 recipe Sicilian-Style Pizza Dough (page 128)

4 ounces fresh mozzarella cheese, cut into 24 equal cubes

Flour for dusting

Extralight olive oil for deep-frying

In a large pot, heat the 4 tablespoons oil over medium heat. Add the celery, carrot, onion, and garlic, and slowly sauté until tender, 6 to 8 minutes. Stir in the basil, parsley, sage, bay leaf, and red pepper flakes. Increase the heat to medium-high and add the ground meat and prosciutto or ham. Cook, stirring often, until the meat starts to brown, 8 to 10 minutes. Add the wine, stirring to dislodge any browned bits from the bottom of the pot. Simmer to reduce the liquid by half, 2 to 3 minutes.

continued

Stir in the Tomato Sauce, tomato paste, stock, salt, and pepper. Bring the mixture to a boil, reduce the heat, and simmer, uncovered, for 30 to 45 minutes. Add the peas during the last 10 minutes of cooking. The sauce should be thick and concentrated. When it is done, remove and discard the bay leaf. Cool to room temperature, or refrigerate overnight.

When the pizza dough has risen, divide it equally into 24 balls roughly 1½ inches in diameter. Press a ball of dough into a 3-inch round and place a heaping tablespoon of the meat sauce and a cube of mozzarella in the center. Pull two opposite sides of the dough up around the sauce and pinch them closed at the top, and repeat with the other two opposite sides to form a little pouch or dumpling. Twist or pinch the edges gently to seal them. Place the dumpling smooth side up on a lightly floured baking sheet. Repeat the process with the remaining ingredients. Cover the dumplings with a dry cloth and let them rise in a draft-free spot for 15 minutes.

Fill a deep-fryer with at least 4 inches of the extralight oil, and heat to 375°. Fry the dumplings, 3 or 4 at a time, until golden brown and puffy, about 1½ minutes on each side. Drain on paper towels, and serve hot.

$\mathcal{F}$ried Pizza Dumplings Stuffed with Spinach, Ricotta, and Roasted Garlic

RAVAZZATE DI MAGRO CON AGLIO ARROSTITO

This is a wonderful vegetarian alternative to the preceding recipe.

MAKES 24 3-TO-4-INCH DUMPLINGS

1 10-ounce box frozen chopped spinach, thawed, or 1 large bunch fresh spinach, blanched and chopped

2 tablespoons olive oil

½ teaspoon salt

½ teaspoon freshly ground black pepper

⅛ teaspoon red pepper flakes

2 tablespoons roasted garlic pulp (see Chef's Tip page 251)

1 egg

1 cup ricotta cheese

1 cup freshly grated provolone cheese

½ cup freshly grated Parmesan cheese

¼ cup freshly grated Romano cheese

1 recipe Sicilian-Style Pizza Dough (page 128)

½ cup Pizza Sauce (page 233)

Flour for dusting

Extralight olive oil for deep-frying

Squeeze out as much water as possible from the spinach. Heat the 2 tablespoons oil in a skillet or sauté pan over medium-high heat. Add the spinach, and sauté until warmed through and tender, 2 to 3 minutes. Season with the salt, pepper, and red pepper flakes, and set aside to cool.

In a large bowl, beat together the roasted garlic pulp, egg, and the four cheeses, and blend until creamy. Stir in the spinach.

When the pizza dough has risen, divide it equally into 24 balls roughly 1½ to 2 inches in diameter. Press or roll a ball of dough into a 3-to-4-inch round, and dollop it with a teaspoon of Pizza Sauce and a tablespoon of the cheese-and-spinach mixture. Fold the dough over to form a half-moon, and seal the edges tightly. Repeat the process with the remaining ingredients. Set the finished dumplings on a cookie sheet or a pizza pan dusted with

continued

PIZZA

flour, cover with a dry cloth, and let them rise in a draft-free spot for 15 minutes.

Fill a deep-fryer with at least 4 inches of the extralight oil, and heat to 375°. Fry the dumplings, 3 or 4 at a time, until golden brown and puffy, about 1½ minutes on each side. Drain on paper towels, and serve hot.

Passione

Garlic-Rosemary Flatbread

PIZZA AGLIATA AL ROSMARINO

This recipe is destined to become a regular at your home. Serve it as an appetizer or in place of bread at your next family meal.

MAKES 2 12-INCH PIZZAS

1 recipe Traditional Pizza Dough (page 127)

Flour or cornmeal for dusting

2 tablespoons olive oil

2 large cloves garlic, chopped

1 teaspoon chopped fresh rosemary

½ teaspoon red pepper flakes

½ teaspoon salt

½ teaspoon freshly ground black pepper

½ cup freshly grated Parmesan cheese

Capers, pitted black olives, and/or diced tomato (optional)

Preheat the oven to 500°. If you are using a pizza stone, place it on a middle rack and preheat it with the oven. If you are using a pizza pan, arrange the rack near the center of the oven.

Divide the pizza dough in half. Pat or roll each half into a 12-inch round. Place on a wooden pizza peel or a pizza pan generously dusted with flour or cornmeal. Spread half the oil evenly over each round. Sprinkle each with half the garlic, rosemary, red pepper flakes, salt, pepper, and Parmesan. Add additional ingredients as desired. Cover the pizza you will not be baking immediately with plastic wrap and refrigerate.

If you are using a pizza stone, slide the pizza directly onto the preheated stone. Otherwise, place the prepared pizza on its pan on the rack. Bake for 8 to 10 minutes, until brown, crisp, and bubbling. Remove from the oven, cut into strips or squares, and serve. Bake the second pizza similarly.

Stuffed Pizza Rounds with Salami and Mushrooms

FAGOTTINI DI PIZZA CON SALAME E FUNGHI DI BOSCO

Fagottini means "little bundles," and these delicious packages will soon become favorite bundles of culinary appreciation.

MAKES 8 4-INCH ROUNDS

2 tablespoons olive oil, plus additional for greasing

½ pound white button mushrooms, sliced

4 ounces salami, chopped

4 large cloves garlic, chopped

½ cup white wine

½ cup ricotta cheese

¾ cup freshly grated Romano cheese

1 whole egg, beaten

¼ teaspoon salt

¼ teaspoon freshly ground black pepper

1 recipe Sicilian-Style Pizza Dough (page 128)

Flour or cornmeal for dusting

1 egg yolk mixed with 1 tablespoon water

Heat the 2 tablespoons oil in a large pan or skillet over medium-high heat. Add the mushrooms and sear, stirring occasionally, until they are brown and have lost most of their water, 3 to 4 minutes. Stir in the salami and garlic, and cook 1 minute. Add the wine, and stir to dislodge any browned bits from the bottom of the pan. Simmer until the liquid has reduced to a glaze, 3 to 5 minutes. Remove from the heat and cool to room temperature.

In a medium bowl, stir together the ricotta, Romano, egg, salt, and pepper.

Preheat the oven to 475°. On a lightly oiled work surface, divide the pizza dough equally into 16 balls. Flatten 8 of the balls into 4-to-5-inch rounds and spread a heaping tablespoon of the cheese mixture in the center of each round. Top each with 2 to 3 tablespoons of the mushroom-and-salami mixture. Flatten the remaining

8 balls of dough and set them over the other rounds. Pull a bit of the bottom dough over the top piece all around, and pinch to seal the edges. Place the rounds on baking sheets or pizza pans dusted with flour or cornmeal.

Bake in the center of the over for 10 to 12 minutes, until golden brown. Brush the tops lightly with the egg-yolk-and-water mixture, and bake 1 minute for a shiny glaze. Transfer to a rack or platter, and serve.

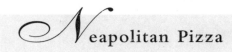

Neapolitan Pizza

PIZZA NAPOLETANA

A simple, traditional pizza—and a perennial favorite.

MAKE 2 14-INCH PIZZAS

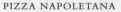

8 ounces fresh mozzarella cheese, diced, plus
    1 cup shredded

1 recipe Traditional Pizza Dough (page 127)

Flour or cornmeal for dusting

½ cup Pizza Sauce (page 233)

6 to 8 anchovy fillets packed in oil, drained
    and chopped

1 cup diced fresh tomato

½ teaspoon dried oregano

¼ teaspoon freshly ground black pepper

Preheat the oven to 500°. If you are using a pizza stone, place it on a middle rack and preheat it with the oven. If you are using a pizza pan, arrange the rack near the center of the oven. If the mozzarella was packed in water, drain it on paper towels while you prepare the other ingredients.

Divide the pizza dough in half. Pat or roll each half into a 14-inch round. Place on a wooden pizza peel or a pizza pan generously dusted with flour or cornmeal.

Spread each evenly with ¼ cup of the Pizza Sauce. Top each with half the anchovy fillets, and sprinkle evenly with half the tomato and half each of the diced and shredded mozzarella. Season each pizza with half each of the oregano and pepper. Cover the pizza you will not be baking immediately with plastic wrap and refrigerate.

If you are using a pizza stone, slide the pizza directly onto the preheated stone. Otherwise, place the prepared pizza in its pan on the rack. Bake for 8 to 10 minutes, until brown, crisp, and bubbling. Remove from the oven, let rest for 1 to 2 minutes, slice into wedges, and serve. Bake the second pizza similarly.

Passione

American-Style Pepperoni Pizza

PIZZA ALL'AMERICANA

There is a difference between American and Italian pizza, and I have never seen this pizza in Italy. But I was instantly taken with American pizza when I came to this country. For your dining pleasure, here's my version of an American classic.

MAKES 2 14-INCH PIZZAS

1 recipe Traditional Pizza Dough (page 127)
Flour or cornmeal for dusting
½ cup Pizza Sauce (page 233)
2 cups shredded mozzarella cheese
2 cups freshly grated Parmesan cheese
¼ teaspoon dried oregano
4 ounces pepperoni sausage, sliced

Preheat the oven to 500°. If you are using a pizza stone, place it on a middle rack and preheat it with the oven. If you are using a pizza pan, arrange the rack in the center of the oven.

Divide the pizza dough in half. Pat or roll each half into a 14-inch round. Place on a wooden pizza peel or a pizza pan generously dusted with flour or cornmeal. Spread ¼ cup of the Pizza Sauce evenly over each round, and distribute the mozzarella, Parmesan, and oregano equally over the sauce. Top each pizza equally with the pepperoni.

If you are using a pizza stone, slide the pizza directly onto the preheated stone. Otherwise, place the prepared pizza on its pan on the rack. Bake for 8 to 10 minutes, until brown, crisp, and bubbling. Remove from the oven, cut into wedges, and serve. Bake the second pizza similarly.

$\mathscr{P}$izza Four Seasons

PIZZA QUATTRO STAGIONI

You'll find this pizza in restaurants all over Italy. While the name re-mains the same, and suggests only four toppings, the rendition differs from region to region. Here is my interpretation, suitable for all seasons.

MAKES 2 14-INCH PIZZAS

8 ounces fresh mozzarella cheese, diced, plus
  ½ cup shredded

1 recipe Traditional Pizza Dough (page 127)

Flour or cornmeal for dusting

½ cup Pizza Sauce (page 233)

1 cup stemmed and sliced shiitake or cremini
  mushrooms

2 ounces prosciutto or ham, thinly sliced and
  julienned

1 9-ounce box frozen artichoke hearts, thawed
  and chopped or 1 14-ounce can, drained,
  rinsed, and chopped

½ cup halved pitted black olives

1 cup diced fresh tomato

¼ teaspoon freshly ground black pepper

¼ teaspoon dried oregano

Preheat the oven to 500°. If you are using a pizza stone, place it on a middle rack and preheat it with the oven. If you are using a pizza pan, arrange the rack near the center of the oven. If the mozzarella was packed in water, drain it on paper towels while you prepare the other ingredients.

Divide the dough in half. Pat or roll each half into a 14-inch round. Place on a wooden pizza peel or a pizza pan gener-ously dusted with flour or cornmeal. Spread each evenly with ¼ cup of the Pizza Sauce. Top each with half the mush-rooms, prosciutto or ham, artichoke hearts, olives, and tomato (see Chef's Tip). Sprinkle each with half each of the diced and shredded mozzarella, and season with half the pepper and oregano. Cover the pizza you will not be baking immediately with plastic wrap and refrigerate.

If you are using a pizza stone, slide the pizza directly onto the preheated stone. Otherwise, place the prepared pizza on its pan on the rack. Bake for 8 to 10 minutes, until brown, crisp, and bubbling. Remove from the oven, let rest for 1 to 2 minutes, slice into wedges, and serve. Bake the second pizza similarly.

Chef's Tip: *A more typical Pizza Quattro Stagioni would feature four toppings on the tomato sauce, each occupying a separate quarter of the pizza (for instance, mozzarella on one, mushrooms on another, prosciutto on a third, artichokes on a fourth). You may separate the various toppings or mix as you please here.*

$\mathcal{P}$izza Margherita

Legend has it that this pizza was created in honor of Margherita of Savoia, queen of Italy, by a Neapolitan baker in 1889. Today, it is the most popular pizza in Italy, its simplicity belying the elegance of its flavors.

MAKES 2 14-INCH PIZZAS

8 ounces fresh mozzarella cheese, diced, plus
    1 cup shredded
1 recipe Traditional Pizza Dough (page 127)
Flour or cornmeal for dusting
½ cup Pizza Sauce (page 233)
½ loosely packed cup torn basil leaves
½ teaspoon freshly ground black pepper

Preheat the oven to 500°. If you are using a pizza stone, place it on a middle rack and preheat it with the oven. If you are using a pizza pan, arrange the rack near the center of the oven. If the mozzarella was packed in water, drain it on paper towels while you prepare the other ingredients.

Divide the dough in half. Pat or roll each half into a 14-inch round. Place on a wooden pizza peel or a pizza pan generously dusted with flour or cornmeal. Spread each evenly with ¼ cup of the Pizza Sauce. Sprinkle each pizza with half each of the diced and shredded mozzarella and half the basil and pepper.

If you are using a pizza stone, slide the pizza directly onto the preheated stone. Otherwise, place the prepared pizza on its pan on the rack. Bake for 8 to 10 minutes, until brown, crisp, and bubbling. Remove from the oven, let rest for 1 to 2 minutes, slice into wedges, and serve. Bake the second pizza similarly.

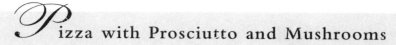

Pizza with Prosciutto and Mushrooms

PIZZA CON PROSCIUTTO E FUNGHI

This recipe brings out the perfect union of prosciutto and mushrooms.

MAKES 2 14-INCH PIZZAS

1 recipe Traditional Pizza Dough (page 127)

Flour or cornmeal for dusting

½ cup Pizza Sauce (page 233)

2 cups sliced white button, cremini, or shiitake mushrooms

1 cup shredded mozzarella cheese

1 cup shredded provolone cheese

2 ounces prosciutto or ham, thinly sliced and cut into ribbons

2 tablespoons chopped fresh basil

4 tablespoons freshly grated Parmesan cheese

½ teaspoon truffle oil (optional)

Preheat the oven to 500°. If you are using a pizza stone, place it on a middle rack and preheat it with the oven. If you are using a pizza pan, arrange the rack near the center of the oven.

Divide the dough in half. Pat or roll each half into a 14-inch round. Place on a wooden pizza peel or a pizza pan generously dusted with flour or cornmeal.

Spread each evenly with ¼ cup of the Pizza Sauce and top with half each of the prepared ingredients in the following order: mushrooms, mozzarella, provolone, prosciutto or ham, and basil. Sprinkle each with half the Parmesan. Cover the pizza you will not be baking immediately with plastic wrap and refrigerate.

If using a pizza stone, slide the pizza directly onto the preheated stone. Otherwise, place the prepared pizza on its pan on the rack. Bake for 8 to 10 minutes, until brown, crisp, and bubbling. Remove from the oven, drizzle with half the truffle oil if desired, slice into wedges, and serve. Bake the second pizza similarly, drizzling with the remaining truffle oil if desired, after baking.

$\mathscr{P}$izza with Caramelized Onion, Roasted Garlic, Prosciutto, and Gorgonzola

PIZZA CON CIPOLLA, AGLIO ARROSTITO, PROSCIUTTO E GORGONZOLA

Some of my favorite ingredients are combined here. This pizza is not for the faint of palate.

MAKES 2 14-INCH PIZZAS

4 tablespoons olive oil

4 cups sliced onion

2 tablespoons roasted garlic pulp (see Chef's Tip page 251)

¼ teaspoon salt

½ teaspoon freshly ground black pepper

1 recipe Traditional Pizza Dough (page 127)

Flour or cornmeal for dusting

4 ounces prosciutto or ham, thinly sliced and cut into ribbons

½ teaspoon dried thyme

¼ teaspoon red pepper flakes

4 ounces Gorgonzola cheese, crumbled

Heat the oil in a large saucepan over medium heat. Stir in the onion and cook, stirring often, until starting to sizzle, 2 to 3 minutes. Reduce the heat and cook slowly until onion is tender and brown, 25 to 30 minutes. Remove the pan from the heat and stir in the roasted garlic pulp. Season with salt and pepper and set aside to cool.

Preheat the oven to 500°. If you are using a pizza stone, place it on a middle rack and preheat it with the oven. If you are using a pizza pan, arrange the rack near the center of the oven.

Divide the dough in half. Pat or roll one each half into a 14-inch round. Place on a wooden pizza peel or a pizza pan generously dusted with flour or cornmeal. Spread each evenly with half the onion mixture, and sprinkle evenly with half each of the prosciutto or ham, thyme, and red pepper flakes. Cover the pizza you will not be baking immediately with plastic wrap and refrigerate.

If you are using a pizza stone, slide the pizza directly onto the preheated stone. Otherwise, place the pizza on its pan on the rack. Bake for 10 to 12 minutes until brown, crisp, and bubbling. Remove from the oven and sprinkle with half the Gorgonzola. Slice into wedges and serve. Bake the second pizza similarly, sprinkling with the remaining Gorgonzola after baking.

$\mathscr{P}$izza with Olives, Capers, and Eggplant

PIZZA CAPONATA

*The popular Sicilian relish caponata, composed of eggplant, onion, and
tomato, makes for an especially flavorful pizza.*

MAKES 2 14-INCH PIZZAS

6 tablespoons olive oil

2 medium eggplants (1 pound each), cut into
    ½-inch cubes

1 cup chopped onion

8 large cloves garlic, thickly sliced

¼ teaspoon red pepper flakes

¼ cup balsamic vinegar

1 cup Tomato Sauce (page 229)

½ cup pitted, halved black olives

¼ cup drained capers

4 tablespoons chopped fresh basil

¼ teaspoon dry oregano

¼ teaspoon freshly ground black pepper

1 recipe Traditional Pizza Dough (page 127)

Flour or cornmeal for dusting

1 cup shredded mozzarella cheese

6 tablespoons freshly grated Romano cheese

In a large skillet or sauté pan, heat half the oil over high heat. Add the eggplant and sear, stirring often, until brown but not tender, 4 to 5 minutes. Remove from the pan with a slotted spoon and set aside. Reduce the heat to medium, add the remaining oil, and slowly cook the onion, garlic, and red pepper flakes until the garlic starts to brown, 2 to 3 minutes. Add the eggplant to the mixture and cook over medium heat until the eggplant is soft, 15 to 18 minutes. Deglaze the pan with the vinegar, stirring to dislodge any browned bits from the bottom. Remove the pan from the heat, and stir in the Tomato Sauce, olives, capers, basil, oregano, and pepper. Cool to room temperature.

Preheat the oven to 500°. If you are using a pizza stone, place it on a middle rack and preheat it with the oven. If you are using a pizza pan, arrange the rack near the center of the oven.

Divide the pizza dough in half. Pat or roll each half into a 14-inch round. Place on a wooden pizza peel or a pizza pan generously dusted with flour or cornmeal. Spread each evenly with half the eggplant mixture, and top with half the mozzarella and half the Romano. Cover the pizza you will not be baking immediately with plastic wrap and refrigerate.

If you are using a pizza stone, slide the pizza directly onto the preheated stone. Otherwise, place the pizza on its pan on the rack. Bake for 8 to 10 minutes, until brown, crisp, and bubbling. Remove from the oven, cut into wedges, and serve. Bake the second pizza similarly.

$\mathscr{P}$izza with Roasted Eggplant, Sausage, and Provolone

PIZZA CON MELANZANA ARROSTITA, SALSICCIA E PROVOLONE

I ran into a version of this pizza while traveling in the southern Italian region of Calabria. The hearty flavor is rustic and soulful at once.

MAKES 2 14-INCH ROUND PIZZAS

6 ounces fresh mozzarella cheese,
    cut into ¼-inch dice

1 medium eggplant (1 pound),
    cut into 1-inch cubes

½ teaspoon salt

3 tablespoons olive oil

1 pound Italian-style sausage, casing removed

1 recipe Traditional Pizza Dough (page 127)

Flour or cornmeal for dusting

½ cup Pizza Sauce (page 233)

6 ounces provolone cheese, half diced,
    half shredded

Preheat the oven to 500°. If you are using a pizza stone, place it on a middle rack and preheat it with the oven. If you are using a pizza pan, arrange the rack near the center of the oven. If the mozzarella was packed in water, drain it on paper towels while you prepare the other ingredients.

Sprinkle the eggplant with the salt and place in a colander. Cover with a dish and put a heavy weight on top. Let the eggplant drain for 15 minutes to remove the bitter juices; pat dry with paper towels.

Toss the eggplant with 2 tablespoons of the oil and spread the cubes in a single layer on a baking sheet. Roast for 10 to 15 minutes, or until well browned and tender. Remove from the baking sheet and cool to room temperature.

Heat the remaining oil in a skillet over medium-high heat. Add the sausage and brown it, breaking it up with a wooden spoon as it cooks. When it is cooked through, drain well on paper towels and set aside.

Divide the pizza dough in half. Pat or roll each half into a 14-inch round. Place on a wooden pizza peel or a pizza pan generously dusted with flour or corn-meal. Spread each evenly with half the Pizza Sauce, and top with half each of the prepared ingredients in the following order: eggplant, diced provolone, sausage, mozzarella, and shredded provolone. Cover the pizza you will not be baking immediately with plastic wrap and refrigerate.

If you are using a pizza stone, slide the pizza directly onto the preheated stone. Otherwise, place the prepared pizza on its pan on the rack. Bake for 8 to 10 minutes, until brown, crisp, and bubbling. Remove from the oven, let cool for 2 to 3 minutes, and slice into wedges and serve. Bake the second pizza similarly.

Pizza with Sausage and Goat Cheese

PIZZA CON SALSICCIA E FORMAGGIO CAPRINO

I learned to appreciate goat cheese later in life. Here is my homage to this tangy variety, which is now one of my favorites.

MAKES 2 14-INCH PIZZAS

1 pound spicy Italian-style sausage, casing removed

1 recipe Traditional Pizza Dough (page 127)

Flour or cornmeal for dusting

½ cup Pizza Sauce (page 233)

8 ounces goat cheese, crumbled

1 cup diced fresh tomato

2 tablespoons chopped fresh basil

½ cup freshly grated provolone cheese

Cook the sausage in a skillet over medium-high heat, breaking it up with a wooden spoon, until it is nicely browned and cooked through, 5 to 6 minutes. Drain on paper towels and set aside.

Preheat the oven to 500°. If you are using a pizza stone, place it on a middle rack and preheat it with the oven. If you are using a pizza pan, arrange the rack near the center of the oven.

Divide the pizza dough in half. Pat or roll each half into a 14-inch round. Place on a wooden pizza peel or a pizza pan generously dusted with flour or cornmeal. Spread each evenly with half the Pizza Sauce. Sprinkle each with half each of the sausage, goat cheese, tomato, and basil, and top with half the grated provolone. Cover the pizza you will not be baking immediately with plastic wrap and refrigerate.

If you are using a pizza stone, slide the pizza directly onto the preheated stone. Otherwise, place the prepared pizza on its pan on the rack. Bake for 8 to 10 minutes, until brown, crisp, and bubbling. Remove from the oven, let rest for 1 to 2 minutes, slice into wedges, and serve. Bake the second pizza similarly.

Pizza with Shrimp, Scallops, and Pancetta

PIZZA MARE E MONTI

Foods from the sea, mare, *and mountains,* monti, *come together here. The various textures and flavors make for a brilliant culinary union.*

MAKES 2 14-INCH PIZZAS

1 cup thinly sliced onion

2 cups water

1 tablespoon vinegar

1 recipe Traditional Pizza Dough (page 127)

Flour or cornmeal for dusting

½ cup Pizza Sauce (page 233)

1 cup shredded mozzarella cheese

4 tablespoons finely chopped fresh basil

½ pound uncooked medium shrimp, peeled, deveined, and chopped into ½-inch pieces

½ pound small bay scallops

4 ounces pancetta or bacon, thinly sliced and chopped

¼ teaspoon red pepper flakes

Extra-virgin olive oil

Finely chopped fresh Italian parsley for garnish

Place the onion in a bowl with the water and vinegar for 15 minutes to lessen the bite of the onion. Drain well and set aside.

Preheat the oven to 500°. If you are using a pizza stone, place it on a middle rack and preheat it with the oven. If you are using a pizza pan, arrange the rack near the center of the oven.

Divide the dough in half. Pat or roll each half into a 14-inch round. Place on a wooden pizza peel or a pizza pan generously dusted with flour or cornmeal. Spread each evenly with ¼ cup of the Pizza Sauce, and top with half each of the mozzarella and basil. Distribute half each of the shrimp, scallops, pancetta or bacon, and onion evenly over each pizza, and sprinkle with half the red pepper flakes. Cover the pizza you will not be baking immediately with plastic wrap and refrigerate.

continued

If you are using a pizza stone, slide the pizza directly onto the preheated stone. Otherwise place the prepared pizza on its pan on the rack. Bake for 10 to 12 minutes, until brown, crisp, and bubbling. Remove from the oven, drizzle with a few drops of the oil, and sprinkle with half the parsley. Slice into wedges and serve. Bake the second pizza similarly, finishing as described above with oil and parsley after baking.

Pizza with Spinach, Tomatoes, and Pine Nuts

PIZZA SAN MARTINO

As kids, my friends and I played poker with pine nuts instead of money. Once, when my family was visiting friends in San Martino, a mountain town near Palermo, my mother used my poker winnings to create this pizza, hence the name.

MAKES 2 14-INCH PIZZAS

1 10-ounce box frozen chopped spinach, thawed

1 tablespoon olive oil

3 large cloves garlic, thickly sliced

1 recipe Traditional Pizza Dough (page 127)

Flour or cornmeal for dusting

½ cup Pizza Sauce (page 233)

½ teaspoon salt

¼ teaspoon freshly ground black pepper

½ cup freshly grated Parmesan cheese

1 cup shredded mozzarella cheese

2 cups sliced fresh Roma tomatoes

¼ cup sliced fresh basil

¼ cup pine nuts

Preheat the oven to 500°. If you are using a pizza stone, place it on a middle rack and preheat it with the oven. If you are using a pizza pan, arrange the rack near the center of the oven.

Squeeze as much water as possible from the spinach. Heat the oil in a skillet over medium-high heat. Add the garlic and cook until it begins to color, 1 minute. Add the spinach and cook for 3 to 5 minutes, until the spinach is tender.

Divide the pizza dough in half. Pat or roll each half into a 14-inch round. Place on a wooden pizza peel or a pizza pan generously dusted with flour or cornmeal. Spread half the Pizza Sauce evenly over each pizza and distribute half the spinach mixture evenly over the sauce. Top each pizza with half each of the Parmesan and

continued

PIZZA

mozzarella, then half each of the tomatoes, basil, and pine nuts. Cover the pizza you will not be baking immediately with plastic wrap and refrigerate.

If you are using a pizza stone, slide the pizza directly onto the preheated stone. Otherwise, place the prepared pizza on its pan on the rack. Bake for 8 to 10 minutes, until brown, crisp, and bubbling. Remove from the oven, cut into wedges, and serve. Bake the second pizza similarly.

Potato Pizza

PIZZA DI PATATE

This adventurous recipe borrows from classic Ligurian cuisine.

1 recipe Traditional Pizza Dough (page 127)

½ cup Pizza Sauce (page 233)

2 small red potatoes, peeled and very thinly sliced

1 cup Ligurian Sauce (page 238)

½ cup freshly grated provolone cheese

Preheat the oven to 500°. If you are using a pizza stone, place it on the middle rack and preheat it with the oven. If you are using a pizza pan, arrange the rack near the center of the oven.

Divide the pizza dough in half. Pat or roll each half into a 14-inch round. Place on a wooden pizza peel or a pizza pan generously dusted with flour or cornmeal. Spread each evenly with ¼ cup of the Pizza Sauce. Arrange half the potato slices evenly over the sauce on each pizza. Dot each equally with small spoonfuls of the Ligurian Sauce and sprinkle with equal amounts of the provolone. Cover the pizza

you will not be baking immediately with plastic wrap and refrigerate.

If you are using a pizza stone, slide the pizza directly onto the preheated stone. Otherwise, place the prepared pizza on its pan on the rack. Bake for 8 to 10 minutes, until brown, crisp, and bubbling. Remove from the oven, let rest for 1 to 2 minutes, slice into wedges, and serve. Bake the second pizza similarly.

PIZZA

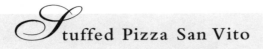

Stuffed Pizza San Vito

SFINCIONE DI SAN VITO

*Like the mythical Sirens, this pizza will captivate anyone who falls under
the spell of its aroma.*

SERVES 6

2 cups Tomato Sauce (page 229)

1 pound Italian-style sausages, casing removed

1 10-ounce box frozen spinach, thawed,
    or 1 large bunch fresh, blanched

2 tablespoons olive oil

4 large cloves garlic, chopped

1½ cups ricotta cheese, drained

1 cup freshly grated Romano cheese

4 ounces salami, chopped

2 raw eggs

½ teaspoon salt

½ teaspoon freshly ground black pepper

Flour or cornmeal for dusting

1 recipe Sicilian-Style Pizza Dough (page 128)

2 hard-boiled eggs, sliced

Simmer the Tomato Sauce and sausage in a medium saucepan for 15 to 20 minutes, until the sausage has cooked through and the sauce has thickened slightly. Cool the sauce to room temperature, remove the sausage, and cut into ½-inch-thick rounds.

Squeeze as much water as possible from the spinach. Heat the oil in a skillet over medium-high heat. Add the spinach and sauté until warmed through and tender, 3 to 4 minutes. Stir in the garlic and cook 1 minute. Set aside to cool.

In a medium bowl, stir together the spinach mixture and the ricotta, Romano, salami, and 1 raw egg. Season with salt and pepper, and set aside.

Preheat the oven to 450°. Dust a large pizza pan with flour or cornmeal. Divide the pizza dough in half. Pat or roll one of the halves into a 14-inch round and place it on the prepared pan. Spoon the sausage and about ½ cup of the sauce from the

Passione

pan evenly over the dough, leaving 1 inch uncovered around the edge. Carefully spread the spinach mixture over the sausage and sauce. Top evenly with the slices of hard-boiled eggs.

Pat or roll the remaining pizza dough into another 14-inch round, and place it over the prepared pizza. Seal by pulling a bit of the bottom dough up over the top and pinching or crimping the two tightly together all around.

Bake in the center of the oven for 18 to 20 minutes, until the dough is crusty and brown, and the filling cooked through. For a glossy brown finish, mix the remaining raw egg with 2 tablespoons of the sauce. Remove the pizza from the oven and brush lightly with the egg-and-sauce mixture. Return to the oven for 2 to 3 minutes to glaze. Remove from the oven and allow to rest for 5 minutes before slicing into wedges. Serve with the remaining sauce on the side.

Stuffed Pizza with Prosciutto, Artichokes, and Three Cheeses

PIZZA RIPIENA DI PROSCIUTTO, CARCIOFI E TRE FORMAGGI

Serve this pizza the next time your whole family gathers at the table, and watch with pride and joy as it disappears before your eyes. The only sounds you will hear are sighs of ecstasy between bites.

SERVES 6 TO 8

1 recipe Sicilian-Style Pizza Dough
    (see page 128)

Flour or cornmeal for dusting

8 ounces prosciutto or ham, cut into ½-inch
    cubes

1 cup shredded mozzarella cheese

½ cup freshly grated Parmesan cheese

½ cup freshly grated provolone cheese

1 9-ounce box frozen artichoke hearts, thawed
    and diced, or 1 14-ounce can, drained,
    rinsed, and diced

1 cup frozen peas, thawed

1 egg yolk mixed with 1 tablespoon water

Preheat the oven to 450°. Place the rack on the lower shelf.

Divide the pizza dough in half. Pat or roll one of the halves into a 14-inch round and place on a pizza pan generously dusted with flour or cornmeal. Sprinkle all the ingredients except the egg-yolk-and-water mixture evenly over the dough, leaving a 1-inch border uncovered around the edge. Pat or roll the remaining dough into another 14-inch round. Place the second piece of dough over the toppings. Seal the pizza by pulling a bit of the bottom up and over the top and pinching or crimping the two tightly together all around.

Bake at the center of the oven for 18 to 20 minutes, until the top is crusty and brown, and the filling cooked through. Brush the top of the pie lightly with the egg-yolk-and-water mixture and return to

Passione

the oven for 1 to 2 minutes to glaze. Remove from the oven, let rest for 5 minutes, slice into wedges, and serve.

Chef's Tip: *To make individual stuffed pizzas, divide the dough equally into 16 balls. Roll or stretch the balls into 4-to-5-inch rounds. Distribute the filling evenly on 8 of the rounds, and top with the remaining rounds of dough. Pinch to seal as for the large pie, and bake on well-floured pizza pans or a preheated pizza stone for 10 to 12 minutes, until brown and crisp. Glaze with the egg-yolk-and-water mixture and return to the oven for 1 minute. Serve hot.*

Stuffed Pizza with Radicchio, Prosciutto, and Camembert

TORTINO DI PIZZA CON RADICCHIO, PROSCIUTTO E CAMEMBERT

I borrowed a proven combination of flavors for this recipe. The cheese, while not Italian, graciously enhances the flavor.

SERVES 6 TO 8

4 tablespoons olive oil

½ cup chopped onion

4 large cloves garlic, thickly sliced

⅛ teaspoon red pepper flakes

2 medium heads radicchio, cored and outer leaves removed, and quartered and sliced into ½-inch-wide ribbons

½ cup white wine

½ cup Chicken Stock (page 223)

1 recipe Sicilian-Style Pizza Dough (page 128)

Flour or cornmeal for dusting

¼ teaspoon salt

¼ teaspoon freshly ground black pepper

8 ounces Camembert, thickly sliced

4 ounces prosciutto or ham, thinly sliced

1 egg yolk mixed with 1 teaspoon tomato paste

2 tablespoons freshly grated Romano cheese

Heat the oil in a large skillet or sauté pan over medium heat. Add the onion, garlic, and red pepper flakes and sauté until the onion is tender and golden brown, 6 to 8 minutes. Add the radicchio and cook until it is lightly brown and wilted, 2 to 3 minutes. Add the wine and simmer until the liquid has reduced completely, 3 to 4 minutes. Add the Chicken Stock and cook until the radicchio is soft and the liquid nearly gone, 3 to 4 minutes. Remove the pan from the heat and season the mixture with the salt and pepper. Cool to room temperature.

Preheat the oven to 450°. Divide the pizza dough in half. Pat or roll one of the halves into a 14-inch round and place it on a pizza pan dusted with flour or cornmeal. Spoon the radicchio mixture evenly over the dough, leaving 1 inch uncovered around the edge. Distribute the Camembert evenly over the radicchio, and top evenly with the prosciutto or ham.

Pat or roll the remaining dough into another 14-inch round and place over the toppings. Seal the pizza by pulling a bit of the bottom up over the top and pinching or crimping the two tightly together all around.

Bake at the center of the oven for 18 to 20 minutes, until the top is crusty and brown. Remove from the oven and brush lightly with the egg-yolk-and-tomato-paste mixture. Sprinkle the top with the Romano and return to the oven for 1 to 2 minutes to glaze. Let cool for at least 5 minutes before slicing into wedges and serving.

Panini

Long before the Earl of Sandwich lent his name to the now ubiquitous combination of bread and filling, Italians were enjoying panini (literally, *panino* means "little bread," and the word may refer also to a roll or bun). Not usually considered meals in themselves, panini are also known as *tramezzini,* or "in-betweens." These small sandwiches are eaten as snacks between breakfast and lunch, or in the afternoon before dinner, which in Italy may not be until eight or nine, or even later.

Throughout Italy today, you can find thriving *paninerie,* or *paninoteche,* shops that specialize in sandwiches, usually accompanied by fine beer or wine sold by the glass.

In this section are a wide variety of panini, both traditional and original versions, including my Hamburger Italiano, which is about as far as you can get from McDonald's fare and still call it a hamburger. You can make these for any occasion when you'd normally be serving sandwiches—lunches, picnics, snacks, casual get-togethers.

A word on toasting: When a recipe calls for toasting bread or rolls, you may do so in a toaster or toaster oven or in a preheated broiler. Sliced rolls may be toasted open or closed, depending on your preference, or as the recipe indicates.

*E*gg Buns

PANINI ALL'UOVO

These delicate buns work well for any sandwich and also make delectable dinner rolls.

½ cup water

½ cup whole milk

1½ tablespoons dry yeast (2 ¼-ounce packages)

1 teaspoon sugar

4 cups all-purpose flour, plus additional for dusting

1½ teaspoons salt

2 eggs, plus 1 large egg beaten with a pinch of salt

1 tablespoon olive oil, plus additional for greasing

Heat the water and milk in a small saucepan until warm but not hot (about 110°). Remove from the heat and stir in the yeast and sugar. Allow the mixture to rest for 5 minutes to bloom.

Combine 3½ cups of the flour and the salt in a large mixing bowl. Stir in the yeast mixture, 2 eggs, and oil. Turn the dough out onto a counter and knead in the remaining flour for about 5 minutes to form a smooth, elastic dough. Place the dough in an oiled bowl and cover with a dry cloth or plastic wrap. Let rise in a warm, draft-free spot until doubled in bulk, about 45 minutes.

Preheat the oven to 375°. Once the dough has risen, turn it out onto a flat surface dusted with flour and cut into 8 equal portions. Roll each into a 6x4-inch rectangle. Roll up the long side to form a thick cigar shape, and pinching the seam to seal it. Pinch the ends and fold under.

Passione

Place the buns seam side down on a heavily floured baking sheet. Cover with plastic wrap and allow to rise until almost doubled in bulk, about 20 minutes.

Once the dough has risen, cut 3 or 4 small slashes into the top of each bun with a sharp knife. Gently brush the buns with the beaten egg, and bake for 35 minutes, or until nicely browned. Remove to a cooling rack.

Sicilian Buns

SFINCIONELLI

This is my version of the dinner rolls that daily graced my family's table.
They accompany any dinner well and also make terrific panini.

MAKES 8 BUNS

1½ cups warm water

1½ tablespoons dry yeast (2 ¼-ounce packages)

1 teaspoon sugar

4 cups all-purpose flour

½ teaspoon salt

1 tablespoon olive oil, plus additional for greasing

1 egg, beaten (optional)

Sesame seeds for sprinkling (optional)

Stir together the water, yeast, and sugar. Set the mixture aside until the yeast blooms, about 5 minutes.

Place 3 cups of the flour and the salt in a mixing bowl. Add the yeast mixture and the oil, and stir to form a sticky dough. Knead, adding the remaining flour a little at a time, until the dough becomes a smooth, elastic ball, about 5 to 8 minutes. If you use an electric mixer, combine the ingredients with the paddle attachment and then change to the dough hook. Add the flour, a little at a time, until the dough is smooth and comes away from the sides of the bowl, about 2 to 4 minutes. Turn the dough into a lightly oiled bowl and cover with a dry cloth or plastic wrap. Let rise in a draft-free spot until doubled in bulk, about 30 minutes.

Preheat the oven to 400°. Once the dough has risen, lift it out and cut into 8 equal balls. Shape into flat 5-inch rounds for buns, or 6-inch oblongs for hero- or hoagie-style rolls. Place on a lightly oiled baking sheet and cover with a dry cloth. Let rise in a draft-free spot for 30 to 45 minutes.

Gently glaze the buns with the egg and sprinkle with the sesame seeds, if desired. Bake for 10 to 12 minutes, until golden brown. Transfer to a cooling rack until ready to use.

*L*amb Meatball Sandwiches with Minted Tomato Sauce

PANINI CON POLPETTINE DI AGNELLO

Mint and lamb are a classic combination. This recipe, which comes from my father's personal collection, is a rendition of a southern Italian sandwich.

MAKES 8 SANDWICHES

1½ pounds ground lamb

¾ cup freshly grated Romano cheese

¾ cup Italian-Style Bread Crumbs (page 220)

2 eggs

8 large cloves garlic, minced

3 tablespoons chopped fresh mint

¾ teaspoon salt

¾ teaspoon freshly ground black pepper

½ teaspoon ground cumin

¼ teaspoon sugar

⅛ teaspoon ground cinnamon

4 tablespoons olive oil

1 cup Beef Stock (page 221)

1 cup Tomato Sauce (page 229)

1 recipe Sicilian Buns (page 176), shaped into 6-inch hero- or hoagie-style rolls

1 cup freshly grated provolone cheese

Preheat the broiler.

In a large bowl, combine the lamb, Romano, bread crumbs, eggs, garlic, 1 tablespoon of the mint, ½ teaspoon each of the salt and pepper, the cumin, sugar, and cinnamon. Knead to form a smooth, well-combined paste. Dampen your hands with water and shape into 24 slightly oblong meatballs, roughly 2 x 1½ inches.

Heat the oil in a large, deep sauté pan over medium-high heat, and brown the meatballs for 5 to 6 minutes. Add the stock, Tomato Sauce, the remaining mint, salt, and pepper, and bring the liquid to a boil. Reduce the heat and simmer until the sauce has thickened slightly and the meatballs are cooked through, 25 to 30 minutes.

Slice the buns not quite all the way through, open slightly, and place 3 meatballs and a few tablespoons of sauce in each. Top this filling with the cheese, close, and place under the broiler until the cheese melts, 1 to 2 minutes. Serve immediately, with additional sauce on the side.

Prosciutto Sandwiches with Mint, Mascarpone, and Parmesan

PANINI DEL COMMENDATORE

*Commendatore is an honorary title in Italy, given to exemplary citizens.
I first saw this honorable sandwich at a sandwich shop near Milan, and
this is my version.*

MAKES 4 SANDWICHES

1 cup frozen lima beans or fava beans

4 hard-boiled egg yolks

½ cup mascarpone cheese

1 tablespoon chopped fresh mint

1 teaspoon pink peppercorns, crushed

½ teaspoon salt

8 slices seedless rye bread

2 large cloves garlic

6 ounces prosciutto or ham, thinly sliced

1 ounce Parmesan cheese, shaved

Cook the beans according to the package directions. When they are tender, drain well and cool to room temperature. Purée in a food processor with the egg yolks, mascarpone, mint, peppercorns, and salt.

Toast the bread. Rub each toasted slice with the garlic, and spread one side of each slice evenly with the bean mixture. Divide the prosciutto or ham equally among 4 slices and top each equally with Parmesan. Close the sandwiches with the remaining slices and serve.

Breaded Ham-and-Cheese Sandwiches

MOZZARELLA IN CARROZZA

This recipe interprets an Italian classic that can be found, with variations, all over the country.

MAKES 4 SANDWICHES

5 large eggs

5 tablespoons water

2 cups Italian-Style Bread Crumbs (page 220)

1 teaspoon paprika

1 teaspoon salt

½ teaspoon freshly ground black pepper

8 slices hearty white bread, cut no more than ½ inch thick, crusts trimmed (a pullman loaf works well)

8 ounces prosciutto or ham, thinly sliced

8 ounces fresh mozzarella cheese, shredded or very thinly sliced (see Chef's Tip)

Extralight olive oil as needed

In a wide, shallow bowl, whisk the eggs with the water.

In a separate wide, shallow bowl or a pie plate, combine the bread crumbs, paprika, salt, and pepper. Place 4 slices of the bread on the work surface. Top each with a quarter each of the prosciutto or ham and mozzarella. Cover each sandwich with a second slice of bread. Push down with your palms to compress the bread, meat, and cheese.

Place a sandwich in the egg mixture and let sit for a few seconds. Turn over and dip the other side. Hold the sandwich over the bowl and drain. Place the egg-dipped sandwich in the bread crumbs. Coat both sides well, patting the crumbs to help them adhere. Repeat the process with the remaining sandwiches.

When all the sandwiches are breaded, heat 3 tablespoons of the oil in a large, deep sauté pan over high heat until very hot.

Reduce the heat to medium-high, and place 2 sandwiches in the oil. Put a heavy weight on top of the sandwiches (a small cast-iron pan will do the job), and cook for 1 to 2 minutes. Remove the weight, turn the sandwiches over, re-place the weight, and cook for another 1 to 2 minutes. The sandwiches should be a dark golden brown outside; on the inside, the prosciutto or ham should be warm and the cheese beginning to melt. Cook the remaining 2 sandwiches the same way, adding more oil to the pan as needed.

Chef's Tip: *If the mozzarella was packed in water, drain on paper towels before shredding or slicing.*

Prosciutto, Pâté, and Camembert Sandwiches

PANINI CON PROSCIUTTO, PÂTÉ E CAMEMBERT

While I usually choose to avoid unnecessary complications, I have become enamored of these little jewels, an affluent version of ham-and-cheese. The preparation is a bit involved, but well worth it.

MAKES 6 SANDWICHES

4 ounces liver pâté

2 ounces cream cheese

¼ teaspoon truffle oil (optional)

6 Egg Buns (page 174) or 6 6-to-8-inch lengths fresh baguette

2 large cloves garlic, peeled

8 ounces Camembert cheese, cut into ½-inch slices

6 ounces prosciutto or ham, thinly sliced

Preheat the broiler for toasting.

In a food processor, purée the pâté, cream cheese, and truffle oil, if desired, to make a smooth spread. Set aside.

Split the buns or baguette pieces in half lengthwise and toast in the broiler until golden brown, 1 to 2 minutes. Rub the toasted interiors of the bread with the garlic. Distribute the Camembert slices equally on the bottom halves of the buns or baguette. Top likewise with the slices of ham. Place the pâté mixture in a pastry bag and pipe it on the ham. Cover with the top halves of the bread and serve.

Chicken Caesar Sandwiches

PANINI DI ZIO CESARE

I always enjoy a good Caesar salad, and here I have incorporated the dressing into my mother's chicken cutlet sandwich.

MAKES 4 SANDWICHES

4 skinless and boneless chicken breast halves (5 to 6 ounces each)

¾ cup all-purpose flour

1 teaspoon salt

½ teaspoon freshly ground black pepper

1 cup bread crumbs

1 tablespoon finely, freshly grated Parmesan cheese

1 tablespoon freshly grated Romano cheese

¼ teaspoon dried thyme

½ teaspoon dried oregano

2 large eggs

4 tablespoons olive oil

4 to 6 large leaves romaine lettuce, washed, dried, and trimmed

8 slices dense sourdough bread, cut ½ inch thick

1 recipe Caesar Sandwich Spread (page 253)

Remove the tenderloin from the pieces of chicken. (You may reserve for another use; see Chef's Tips.) Place the chicken between pieces of wax paper and pound to about ¼ inch thick (not any thinner).

In a bowl, combine the flour, salt, and pepper well. In another bowl, combine the bread crumbs, cheeses, and herbs well. Place the eggs in a third bowl and whisk well.

Dip a piece of chicken in the whisked eggs to coat it completely. Lift out, letting the excess egg drip back into the bowl. Transfer the chicken to the flour mixture, and turn it so both sides are covered. Shake off the excess flour. Dip the chicken again in the egg mixture and let the excess drip off quickly. Place the chicken in the bread crumb mixture and coat well, spooning crumbs over the top and patting well to form a solid coating all over. Remove the coated chicken to a clean plate, and repeat with the remaining chicken.

continued

P A N I N I

In a large, deep sauté pan, heat 3 tablespoons of the oil over medium-high heat. When the oil is hot, add 2 pieces of chicken (do not crowd the pan), and sauté until well browned on both sides, about 2 to 3 minutes per side. Add 1 more tablespoon oil and repeat with the remaining chicken. Cut each cooked piece on the diagonal into ½-inch-wide slices.

Lay out two slices of bread per sandwich. Spread 2 teaspoons of the Caesar Sandwich Spread on each slice. Place the slices from 1 piece of chicken on top of 1 slice of bread, and spoon 1 to 2 more teaspoons of sauce on top of the chicken. Top with 1 or 2 pieces of romaine lettuce, cut to fit, and cover with a second slice of bread. Repeat with the remaining ingredients.

Chef's Tips: *For a delicious variation of this sandwich, cut roasted red peppers (fresh or from a jar) into ¼-inch strips; you'll want about 4 table-spoons total, 1 tablespoon per sandwich. If using peppers from a jar, rinse and dry well. Place the peppers in a small bowl, and sprinkle with ½ to 1 teaspoon balsamic vinegar. Add the peppers to the sandwich between the chicken and lettuce.*

You can bread and sauté the tenderloins in the same way as you do the breasts. They make a nice hors d'oeuvre, served with your favorite dipping sauce.

Turkey Meatball Sandwiches with Cream Sauce

PANINI CON POLPETTE DI TACCHINO ALLA CREMA

You could easily transform this sandwich into a main meal by omitting the bread and serving the meatballs with a side of mashed potatoes.

MAKES 4 SANDWICHES

¾ pound ground turkey (see Chef's Tip)

4 cloves garlic, minced, plus 1 whole clove, peeled

2 tablespoons diced white onion

½ cup bread crumbs

4 tablespoons heavy cream

1 large egg

2 tablespoons freshly grated Romano cheese

3 tablespoons chopped fresh Italian parsley

2 tablespoons chopped fresh oregano

1½ teaspoons salt

2 cups Chicken Stock (page 223)

1½ cups whole milk, or ¾ cup heavy cream mixed with ¾ cup water

3 tablespoons unsalted butter, softened

2 tablespoons all-purpose flour

¼ teaspoon freshly ground black pepper

½ teaspoon paprika

1 tablespoon freshly grated Parmesan cheese

4 soft hero rolls or 8 slices dense sourdough bread

1 small red bell pepper, cut into ¼-inch dice

Preheat the broiler for toasting.

Place the turkey, minced garlic, onion, bread crumbs, cream, egg, Romano, 2 tablespoons of the parsley, 1 tablespoon of the oregano, and 1 teaspoon of the salt in a bowl. With clean hands, gently combine the ingredients until well blended. Do not overblend. Divide the mixture into 8 equal portions and gently form each into a meatball about 2 inches in diameter.

In a medium saucepan, bring the stock and the milk or cream-and-water mixture to a boil. Add the meatballs, reduce the heat, and simmer for 20 to 25 minutes, until the meatballs are cooked through. Remove the meatballs with a slotted spoon and set aside. Bring the liquid back to a boil and reduce until just 2 cups remain, about 5 to 8 minutes.

continued

Meanwhile, melt the butter in a separate saucepan over low heat. Add the flour and whisk until it is fully incorporated. Slowly add the 2 cups of warm reduced liquid, whisking constantly. Add the remaining parsley, oregano, and salt, and the pepper and paprika. Cook, whisking, until the sauce begins to thicken, about 10 minutes. Stir in the Parmesan and remove the pan from the heat.

Slice open the rolls, if using, and lightly toast the rolls or bread in a toaster oven or the broiler. Rub the toasted interiors of the rolls or one side of each slice of bread with the garlic clove. Spoon 2 teaspoons of the sauce over each of the interior surfaces. Slice 2 meatballs per sandwich and place the slices on the sauce. Top with a few more teaspoons of sauce and a generous sprinkling of bell pepper. Cover with the other side of the roll or the second slice of bread. Serve immediately, with any extra sauce passed warm at the table for dipping.

Chef's Tip: *You may use ground chicken in place of turkey.*

Chicken Salad Sandwiches

PANINI CON INSALATA DI POLLO

Are you tired of the same old chicken salad sandwich? Try this, and you will have a new appreciation for a classic.

MAKES 4 LARGER OR 6 SMALLER
SANDWICHES

4 cups Chicken Stock (page 223)

1 carrot, peeled, trimmed, and cut into chunks

1 stalk celery, trimmed and cut into chunks, plus 2 stalks from the heart or 1 large staik, cut into ¼-inch dice

1 small onion, peeled and cut into chunks

2 tablespoons Italian parsley leaves, rinsed and dried (optional)

2 large skinless and boneless chicken breast halves (1 pound total; see Chef's Tip)

½ cup mayonnaise

1½ tablespoons honey mustard, or 1 tablespoon Dijon mustard mixed with 2 teaspoons honey

¼ pound honey- or sweet-baked ham, cut into ¼-inch dice

1 7.75-ounce can hearts of palm, drained and cut into ¼-inch rounds

4 large hero rolls or 6 smaller rolls

Inner leaves from 1 small cored head radicchio, washed, dried, and separated

Preheat the broiler for toasting.

Place the stock, carrot, chunked celery, onion, and parsley, if using, in a large, deep sauté pan or a 2-quart saucepan. Add enough water to make the liquid 2 inches deep, bring the liquid to a boil, and reduce to a low simmer. Add the chicken and simmer on low for 10 to 14 minutes, turning the chicken once halfway through the cooking time, which will depend on the thickness of the meat and the intensity of the simmer. Cut into the chicken after 8 to 10 minutes to check the color; it should be white throughout, with no pink. When the chicken breasts have finished cooking, remove from the liquid with a slotted spoon and set aside to cool. When the chicken is cool enough to handle, cut into ½-inch dice and place in a medium glass bowl. You should have about 2 to 2¼ cups of diced chicken.

continued

PANINI

Combine the mayonnaise and honey mustard. Add 5 tablespoons of this mixture, and the ham, hearts of palm, and diced celery to the chicken, and mix well.

Split the rolls along the side without separating them completely, and open gently. Toast in the broiler. Spread the toasted interiors equally with the remaining mayonnaise mixture. Place equal portions of the chicken salad on the bottom halves of the rolls, and top with 1 or 2 radicchio leaves each. Cover with the top halves and serve.

Chef's Tip: *You may substitute store-bought roast chicken for the poached breasts. Remove the skin and bones and dice to obtain 2 to 2¼ cups of the breast meat. You won't need the poaching ingredients (stock, carrot, onion, chunked celery, parsley) and can avoid the entire poaching process. If using roast chicken, you may need to add a bit more mayonnaise and honey mustard, as the roast meat may be drier than poached.*

Fried Eggplant Sandwiches

PANINI CON MELANZANE FRITTE

This sandwich could rival pizza as one of southern Italy's most popular culinary exports.

MAKES 4 SANDWICHES

1 eggplant (about ¾ to 1 pound)

Coarse salt

¾ cup all-purpose flour

1 teaspoon salt

½ teaspoon freshly ground black pepper

1 teaspoon garlic powder

1 cup bread crumbs

2 tablespoons finely chopped toasted pine nuts
    (see Chef's Tips page 199)

2 tablespoons freshly grated Romano cheese

2 large eggs

2 cups Tomato Sauce (page 229), warmed

6 to 8 large basil leaves, thinly sliced

4 to 6 tablespoons olive oil

1 packed cup shredded mozzarella cheese

¼ packed cup freshly grated Parmesan cheese

4 Egg Buns (page 174) or other soft rolls,
    about 4 inches across

1 whole clove garlic, peeled

Peel the eggplant and cut off the ends, and slice the eggplant crosswise into pieces about ¼ but no more than ½ inch thick. Lay the slices on a baking sheet lined with plastic wrap. Sprinkle generously with the coarse salt, and let sit for 45 minutes. The salt will help draw the bitter juice from the eggplant. After the 45 minutes, pat the eggplant dry with paper towels to absorb all the liquid.

Meanwhile, combine the flour, salt, pepper, and garlic powder in a shallow bowl or a pie plate. Combine the bread crumbs, pine nuts, and Romano in a second shallow bowl or pie plate. In another bowl, whisk the eggs well.

Place the Tomato Sauce and basil in a saucepan. Bring to a boil; then reduce the heat and keep the sauce at a low simmer while you prepare the eggplant. Dip a slice of eggplant in the eggs, letting any excess

continued

PANINI

drip into the bowl. Transfer the eggplant to the flour mixture and coat both sides. Gently shake off the excess. Dip again in the eggs, letting the excess drip off quickly. Place the floured eggplant in the bread crumb mixture, and pat the crumbs in firmly on both sides. Place the coated slice of eggplant on a plate or tray. Repeat the process with the remaining slices.

Preheat the broiler.

In a wide sauté pan, heat 4 tablespoons of the oil over medium-high heat. When the oil is hot, put in a few slices of the coated eggplant. Do not crowd the pan. Fry the slices until dark golden brown on both sides, about 2 to 3 minutes per side. Remove the slices to a baking sheet lined with foil as they are done. Add 2 tablespoons of the oil if necessary, and fry the remaining eggplant.

Distribute the mozzarella and Parmesan evenly on top of the eggplant. Broil for about 2 minutes, until the cheese is melted. Be careful that the eggplant does not burn.

Slice the buns or rolls open and toast lightly. Gently rub the toasted interiors of the buns or rolls with the garlic. Spread 1 or 2 teaspoons of the Tomato Sauce on each interior face. Distribute the eggplant slices equally among the bottoms of the buns or rolls, layering as necessary to fit. Top the eggplant with 2 teaspoons of sauce per bun, and cover with the tops of the buns. Serve immediately, with any extra sauce passed warm at the table for dipping.

Fontina, Mushroom, and Truffle Sandwiches

PANINI ELEGANTI

I had a version of this sandwich in the Emilia-Romagna region. I loved it so much that I tried to re-create it on my return to the States.

MAKES 4 SANDWICHES

MUSHROOM SPREAD

¾ cup Chicken Stock (page 223)

½ ounce dried porcini mushrooms

2 tablespoons olive oil

½ pound mixed cremini and white button mushrooms, sliced

4 cloves garlic, thickly sliced

2 tablespoons chopped fresh Italian parsley

4 ounces mascarpone or cream cheese

¾ teaspoon Worcestershire sauce

¼ teaspoon truffle oil

1 tablespoon brandy

8 slices egg bread, or 4 Egg Buns (page 174) or soft ciabatta rolls, sliced open

24 to 32 whole Italian parsley leaves, rinsed and dried

1 small fresh black truffle, shaved (see Chef's Tips)

FONTINA CREAM

3 tablespoons heavy cream

4 ounces Fontina cheese, shredded (Gruyère may be substituted)

2 teaspoons brandy

Make the mushroom spread: In a small saucepan, heat the stock to a boil. Turn off the heat and add the dried porcini. Let sit for 4 to 5 minutes, until softened. Drain the mushrooms, reserving the liquid. Roughly chop the porcini and set aside.

Preheat the broiler for toasting.

In a large, deep sauté pan, heat the oil. Add the cremini and white button mushrooms and porcini, and sauté over medium-high heat for 4 to 7 minutes. Add the garlic and chopped parsley. Stir well and cook for 1 to 2 minutes. Add the reserved stock, stir well, and cook until the liquid is reduced to a glaze and the pan is dry, about 3 to 5 minutes.

In the bowl of a food processor, combine three-fourths of the mushroom mixture, cheese, Worcestershire sauce, truffle oil, and brandy. Process for about 30 seconds.

continued

PANINI

Scrape down the sides of the bowl and process again until the mixture is completely blended. Transfer to a bowl and refrigerate until chilled and set.

Toast the bread or open rolls in the broiler. Have everything else ready for the sandwich assembly—the bread toasted, the mushroom spread chilled, the parsley leaves rinsed and dried, the truffles shaved—before you make the Fontina cream.

Make the Fontina cream: In the top of a double boiler, over simmering (not boiling) water, warm the cream. Add the Fontina and the brandy. Stir until the cheese is melted and well combined with the cream, 1 to 2 minutes. Turn off the heat, and leave the mixture in the top of the double boiler over the hot water.

Assemble the sandwiches: Spread 1 to 2 tablespoons of the chilled mushroom mixture on 4 slices of the toasted bread or the bottom halves of the buns or rolls. Place ¼ of the remaining fourth of the sautéed mushroom mixture on top of the mushroom spread. Place 6 to 8 parsley leaves over the mushrooms, and top with a few truffle shavings. Spread 1 to 2 tablespoons of the Fontina cream on the other slices of the bread or the top halves of the buns, and cover the sandwiches.

Chef's Tips: *If you can't find a fresh truffle, one from a jar or can will do. The mushroom mixture, sprinkled with parsley or topped with a shaving of truffle, can be used as a spread for crostini or canapés.*

$\mathcal{H}$amburgers Italiano

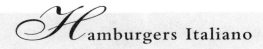

HAMBURGER ALL' ITALIANA

When I came to the States, I fell in a big way for hamburgers. Experimenting with leftovers from my refrigerator, I ended up with this version of the all-American sandwich.

MAKES 4 SANDWICHES

¼ pound sliced pepperoni sausage

¼ pound spicy Italian-style sausage, casing removed

¼ pound ground lamb

¼ pound ground veal

2 egg yolks

¾ cup bread crumbs

¼ cup freshly grated Romano cheese

4 hamburger buns, or soft kaiser or onion rolls, sliced open

1 clove garlic, peeled

4 thin slices sweet onion

4 ounces provolone cheese, sliced

4 thin slices fresh tomato

Preheat the broiler.

Process the pepperoni in the food processor until finely minced. Combine it with the sausage, lamb, veal, egg yolks, bread crumbs, and Romano. Do not overmix. With clean hands, loosely form 4 hamburger patties, ¼ inch thick. Place on a broiler pan and broil for 4 to 5 minutes per side, until cooked through.

Toast the buns or rolls lightly, and rub the toasted interiors gently with the garlic. Place a slice of onion on the bottom half of each bun or roll. Top each with a burger, and top each burger with a quarter of the provolone and a slice of tomato.

Chef's Tip: *These are moist burgers with a kick. If you can't find spicy sausage, use sweet and add ¼ to ½ teaspoon red pepper flakes when combining the meats.*

ℳeatloaf Sandwiches

PANINI CON POLPETTONE

Polpettone, or meatloaf, has long been a culinary lifesaver for many busy cooks. Here is my version of my grandmother's recipe.

MAKES 4 SANDWICHES

½ pound ground pork

½ pound ground veal

½ pound ground lamb

2 raw eggs

⅓ cup chopped fresh Italian parsley

¾ cup freshly grated Romano cheese, plus 4 to 6 teaspoons freshly grated Romano or Parmesan

¾ cup Italian-Style Bread Crumbs (page 220) or coarse fresh bread crumbs

1 teaspoon salt

½ teaspoon freshly ground black pepper

4 ounces soppressata or salami, thinly sliced and chopped into ¼-to-½-inch pieces

4 hard-boiled eggs

⅔ cup tomato ketchup

8 slices dense sourdough or hearty country bread

1 whole clove garlic, peeled

4 ounces provolone cheese, thinly sliced

Preheat the oven to 350°.

With clean hands, combine ground meats, raw eggs, parsley, ½ cup of the Romano, the bread crumbs, salt, and pepper in a large bowl. Mix well but do not overmix or knead, as this can make the meatloaf tough. Place a third of the mixture in the bottom of a 9x5x3- or 8½x4½x2½-inch loaf pan and gently pat into the corners, creating a flat surface. Do not compress the meat too much.

Sprinkle the soppressata or salami over the meat mixture. Line up the hard-boiled eggs, end to end down the center of the pan, on top of the soppressata. Top with the remaining meat mixture. Pat gently around the eggs, filling in to form a flat-topped loaf.

Combine ⅓ cup of the ketchup with ¼ cup of the Romano, and spread the mixture over the top of the meatloaf. Bake until an internal thermometer registers

Passione

155°, about 1 hour. Remove the meatloaf from the oven and let rest for
10 minutes.

Cut four ½-inch-thick slices out of the meatloaf; you will see a cross-section of
the soppressata and egg. Refrigerate the rest of the loaf for more sandwiches or
later meals.

Toast the bread and rub each slice gently with the garlic. Place a slice of meatloaf
on each of 4 slices of the bread. Top each with a quarter of the provolone slices.
Spread 1 to 1½ tablespoons of the remaining ketchup on the other 4 slices of
bread, sprinkle with 1 to 1½ teaspoons of the remaining grated cheese, and
cover each sandwich.

Chef's Tip: *For a tasty variation, sauté ½ cup chopped onion and 2 or 3
cloves garlic, finely minced, with a pinch of red pepper flakes in 1 tablespoon hot olive oil. When this cools, combine it with the rest of the meatloaf ingredients by hand, and proceed with the recipe.*

Portobello Mushroom and Cheese Sandwiches

PANINI CON FUNGHI E FORMAGGIO

Grilled mushroom caps can be as tasty as steak. This recipe will please all those who keep a vegetarian diet, and pleasantly surprise those who don't.

MAKES 4 SANDWICHES

¾ pound large portobello mushroom caps

½ cup olive oil

2 tablespoons balsamic vinegar

3 tablespoons freshly squeezed lemon juice

1 teaspoon finely chopped fresh rosemary

2 teaspoons coarse salt

8 slices dense sourdough bread, or 4 small, soft kaiser or egg rolls, sliced open (you may use Egg Buns, page 174)

1 whole clove garlic, peeled

8 teaspoons pesto sauce

6 to 8 ounces Asiago cheese, thinly sliced (see Chef's Tip)

Preheat the oven to 450°.

Brush the mushroom caps gently to remove any dirt, and cut them into ½-inch-thick slices. Place in a large bowl. In a separate bowl, combine the oil, vinegar, lemon juice, and rosemary, and whisk well. Pour this mixture over the sliced mushrooms, and toss well, until the mushrooms are evenly coated. Let sit for 15 to 30 minutes.

Spread the mushrooms on a baking sheet in a single layer. Sprinkle the salt evenly over them, and roast until softened but still holding their shape, about 10 to 12 minutes.

Toast the bread or rolls lightly. When toasted, gently rub the slices or the interior of the rolls with the garlic.

Preheat the broiler.

Spread 1 teaspoon of the pesto over each slice or the interiors of the rolls. Distribute

Passione

a quarter of the mushrooms over each of 4 slices of bread or the bottom halves of rolls, and cover with a quarter of the Asiago. Place the open sandwich halves under the broiler for 1 to 2 minutes, until the cheese is just melted. Be careful that it does not burn. Cover the sandwiches with the remaining slices of bread or top halves of rolls, and serve immediately.

Chef's Tip: *You can make these sandwiches with fresh water-packed mozzarella instead of Asiago, but the Asiago has more flavor. If using water-packed mozzarella, drain it on paper towels before slicing.*

Prosciutto and Asparagus Cream Sandwiches

PANINI AL PROSCIUTTO CON CREMA D'ASPARAGI

This recipe typifies the unusual combinations found in many new Italian sandwich shops.

MAKES 4 SANDWICHES

1 pound fresh asparagus

1½ teaspoons salt

2 tablespoons olive oil

¼ teaspoon freshly ground black pepper

2 cloves garlic, thickly sliced

2 tablespoons toasted pine nuts
  (see Chef's Tips)

¼ teaspoon red pepper flakes

3 tablespoons white wine

2 tablespoons Chicken Stock (page 223)

2 ounces mascarpone or cream cheese, cut
  into 3 equal chunks

2 tablespoons freshly grated Parmesan cheese

4 ciabatta rolls, 4 to 5 inches long, or 4 such
  lengths soft baguette

1 whole clove garlic, peeled

8 ounces prosciutto or ham, very thinly sliced

4 large leaves romaine lettuce

Cut or snap off the woody ends of the stalks and discard. If the spears are thick, peel the lower parts with a vegetable peeler. Place the trimmed spears in a single layer in a large, deep sauté pan, and add just enough water to cover them, and 1 teaspoon of the salt. Bring the water to a boil, reduce the heat, and simmer until the spears are fork-tender, about 5 minutes (the time will depend on the thickness of the spears). Remove the asparagus from the pan, discard the water, and wipe the pan dry. Cut the tips off the spears and set aside, and cut the remainder of the stalks into ½-inch pieces.

In the dry pan, heat the oil over medium-high heat. Add the ½-inch pieces of asparagus, the remaining salt, the pepper, garlic, pine nuts, and red pepper flakes, and sauté for 3 to 4 minutes. Add the wine and cook for 2 to 3 minutes to reduce most of the liquid. Add the stock and cook to reduce for another 2 to 3 minutes. When most of the liquid has been cooked away, turn off the heat. Transfer the contents of the pan to the bowl of a food processor and process for 30 seconds. Scrape down the sides of the bowl, add the mascarpone or cream cheese, and process until well combined. Add the Parmesan and process until well combined. Refrigerate the mixture until cool; you should have about 1 generous cup.

Now assemble the sandwiches: Slice the rolls or pieces of baguette in half lengthwise, open, and toast lightly. When toasted, gently rub the interiors with the garlic. Spread 1 tablespoon of the asparagus cream on the interior of each roll. Divide half the prosciutto or ham equally among the bottom halves of the rolls, folding the slices to create a ribbon effect. Dab a bit more of the asparagus cream on top, and above that distribute the reserved asparagus tips. Top equally with the remaining prosciutto or ham, folded as above, then the lettuce, torn to fit the rolls. Cover with the top halves of the rolls and serve.

Chef's Tips: *To toast pine nuts, toss them in a little olive oil and bake on a nonstick baking sheet in a preheated 325° oven for 5 to 6 minutes, until light golden brown.*

For nice hors d'oeuvre, if you have any leftover asparagus cream, spread it on crostini, and top with an asparagus tip or a sprinkle of Parmesan.

Salami and Olive-Caper Cream Cheese Sandwiches

PANINI AL SALAME CON CREMA DI CAPPERI E OLIVE

I'm pretty sure you won't see this sandwich at your local deli.

MAKES 4 SANDWICHES

4 kaiser, hero, or ciabatta rolls

1 clove garlic, peeled

1 recipe Olive-Caper Cream Cheese Spread (page 255)

Scant 8 ounces sweet soppressata or salami, thinly sliced

4 ounces provolone, sliced

Slice the rolls lengthwise, open each like a book, and toast lightly. Rub the garlic clove gently over the interiors.

Spread 1 to 2 generous tablespoons of the olive-caper spread over the interiors of each roll. Divide the soppressata or salami and the provolone in 4 equal portions. Roll or fold half the soppressata for each sandwich and place on the olive-caper spread on the bottom half of each roll. Roll or fold the provolone slices and place atop the soppressata, and roll or fold the remaining soppressata and place atop the provolone. Cover with the tops of the rolls and serve.

Chef's Tip: *For a tasty hors d'oeuvre, if you have any leftover olive-caper spread, put it on crostini and top with a small piece of rolled salami or a sprinkle of parsley.*

Stuffed Pizza San Vito

 Prosciutto and Asparagus Cream Sandwich

 Sausage, Pepper, and Onion Sandwich

Chicken Caesar Sandwich

*S*andwiches Tartare

PANINI CON CARNE ALLA TARTARA

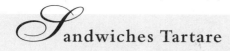

Here's an interesting sandwich for the die-hard fans of steak tartar. Note that these are raw-meat sandwiches; prepare this dish only if you are assured of the cleanliness and quality of the uncooked beef you are using.

MAKES 4 SANDWICHES

8 tablespoons whipped unsalted butter, softened

1¼ teaspoons anchovy paste

½ pound raw, tartare-quality ground beef

1 large egg yolk

1 tablespoon tiny drained capers

2 tablespoons finely diced onion

1½ tablespoons finely chopped pimiento-stuffed green olives

2 tablespoons chopped fresh Italian parsley

¼ teaspoon sweet paprika

1 teaspoon honey mustard

4 Egg Buns (page 174) or soft hamburger buns

1 whole clove garlic, peeled

1 small lemon, cut into 4 wedges

Baby salad greens, washed and dried

Mix the butter with 1 teaspoon of the anchovy paste until well blended and smooth. Set aside.

Combine the beef, egg yolk, capers, onion, olives, parsley, paprika, honey mus-tard, and the remaining anchovy paste until the ingredients are well incorporated. Form the mixture into 4 delicate patties.

Slice the rolls or buns open, and toast. Rub the toasted interiors gently with the garlic, and spread the butter mixture equally on them.

Place one meat patty on the bottom half of each roll or bun. Squeeze a lemon wedge on the meat, and cover with baby greens. Close each sandwich with the top half of the roll or bun, and serve.

Chef's Tips: *Served on small, soft rolls, these are light sandwiches. If you prefer something heartier, make 2 or 3 larger patties and serve them on larger rolls.*

For additional sweetness, add 1 to 2 tablespoons of chopped sweet pickle to the meat mixture.

$\mathcal{S}$ausage, Pepper, and Onion Sandwiches

PANINI CON SALSICCIA, PEPERONE E CIPOLLA

This is a favorite on both sides of the Atlantic. While attending college in the States, I often entertained my friends with these hearty sandwiches, which reminded me of summer barbecues in Sicily.

MAKES 4 SANDWICHES

4 tablespoons olive oil

1 pound sweet Italian sausage (about 6 fat links), casing removed

4 cloves garlic, thickly sliced

¼ teaspoon red pepper flakes

1 small sweet onion, sliced into ¼-inch-thick rings

1 medium red, 1 medium yellow, and 1 medium orange bell pepper, each sliced into ½-inch-wide strips (see Chef's Tip)

½ teaspoon salt

½ cup white wine

¾ cup Chicken Stock (page 223)

4 kaiser rolls

1 whole clove garlic, peeled

Heat 2 tablespoons of the oil in a large, deep sauté pan over medium-high heat. Add the sausage and sauté until well browned on all sides, about 5 minutes. Remove with a slotted spoon, and when cool enough to handle, slice into ½-inch coins. They will still be pink inside.

Add the remaining oil to the same pan, and the garlic, red pepper flakes, onion, bell peppers, and salt. Sauté over medium-high heat until the vegetables are soft, about 8 minutes. Return the sausage to the pan.

Add the wine and stock. The liquid may not completely cover the sausage. Bring the liquid to a boil, lower the heat, and simmer for 7 to 8 minutes. Stir occasionally to turn and coat the ingredients. The sauce should become a thick glaze over the sausages and vegetables.

Slice open the rolls, and toast. Rub the interiors gently with the garlic clove. Spoon equal amounts of the sausage mixture on the bottom halves of the rolls. Cover each with the top half and serve.

Chef's Tip: *To cut a bell pepper, stand it on its end, with the stem up. Slice down four sides of the pepper, beginning just outside the stem. You will have 4 clean quarters, with the stem and core in one piece to be discarded. Cut each of the 4 quarters into ½-inch-wide strips.*

Sausage and Provolone Sandwiches with Tomato Sauce

PANINI CON SALSICCIA E PROVOLONE AL SUGO

This panino may have roots in Italy, but it has become standard in Italian delis in the States. The unforgettable flavor loses nothing in the translation.

MAKES 4 SANDWICHES

2 tablespoons olive oil

1 pound spicy Italian-style sausage (about 6 fat links), casing removed

4 large cloves garlic, thickly sliced

1 cup diced sweet onion

1 cup Tomato Sauce (page 229)

¾ cup Chicken Stock (page 223)

¼ packed cup chopped fresh Italian parsley

4 hero rolls, about 6 inches long

8 heaping tablespoons freshly shredded or grated provolone cheese

2 teaspoons freshly grated Parmesan cheese

In a large, deep sauté pan, heat the olive oil over medium-high heat. Add the sausage and brown well on all sides, about 6 minutes. Remove with a slotted spoon, and when cool enough to handle, slice the links in half lengthwise.

In the same pan, also over medium-high heat, sauté the garlic and onion until softened, about 4 to 5 minutes. Add the Tomato Sauce, stock, and parsley, and stir to combine. Place the sausage in the sauce, cut side down, and let simmer about 30 minutes, until the sausage is cooked through. The sauce should be thickened and cling to the sausage. Keep the sausage and sauce warm over a very low heat as you prepare the bread.

Preheat the broiler. Slice each roll lengthwise, from top to bottom, stopping about three-quarters to the bottom—do not slice all the way through. The rolls should look like hot dog buns. Open each roll, and press down on the soft interior to create a larger pocket. Sprinkle 1 tablespoon of the provolone and ¼ teaspoon of the Parmesan into the pocket of each roll. Top the cheese with 3 sausage halves (a quarter of the sausage pieces) per roll and equal amounts of the sauce. Sprinkle the remaining provolone and Parmesan equally on top, and place the sandwiches on a baking sheet. Broil until the cheese melts, about 1 minute, being careful that the sandwiches do not burn. Serve immediately.

Chef's Tip: *If you can't find spicy sausage, use sweet and add ¼ to ½ teaspoon red pepper flakes, depending on how spicy you like your food, to the garlic-and-onion sauté.*

$\mathscr{S}$hrimp Cake Sandwiches with Tartar Sauce

PANINI CON FRITTELLE DI GAMBERI

This sandwich has an especially delicate texture. The flavor will appeal to anyone who likes shrimp.

MAKES 4 SANDWICHES

1 pound uncooked medium shrimp, peeled and deveined

¼ cup brandy

½ cup heavy cream

¾ teaspoon salt

2 pinches freshly ground black pepper

¼ cup chopped green onion

1 tablespoon finely grated lemon zest

2 eggs

¾ cup Italian-Style Bread Crumbs (page 220)

1 tablespoon freshly grated Romano cheese

½ cup all-purpose flour

6 tablespoons olive oil

8 wide slices challah or egg bread, or 4 Egg Buns (page 174), prepared larger

1 recipe Tartar Sauce (page 254)

½ cucumber, peeled and thinly sliced

Place the shrimp in a glass or porcelain bowl. Pour the brandy, cream, ½ teaspoon of the salt, a pinch of pepper, and the green onion over the shrimp. Toss to coat the shrimp, cover the mixture, and let sit for about 30 minutes. After that time, spoon the solid part of the mixture into the bowl of a food processor, with roughly 2 tablespoons of the liquid, leaving the remaining liquid behind. Pulse three or four times to chop the shrimp, but do not overprocess; the shrimp should be chopped not puréed. Transfer the mixture to a bowl, and stir in the lemon zest.

Whisk the two eggs well in a small glass bowl. Place the bread crumbs on a plate, and mix in the remaining salt and pepper and the Romano.

Divide the shrimp mixture into 8 equal portions. Flour your hands generously and form each portion of the shrimp mixture into a ½-inch-thick patty. Dip each patty into the eggs, coat both sides, and allow any excess to drip off. Transfer each patty to the plate of bread crumbs and coat both sides well. Place the patties on a lightly floured plate or platter as they are done.

In a large deep sauté pan, heat 3 tablespoons of the oil over medium-high heat. Add 4 of the patties and sauté until golden brown and cooked through, about 3 to 4 minutes on each side. Check inside one of the patties to make sure it is cooked through. Remove the patties as they are done to a plate lined with paper towels. Add the remaining oil to the pan and cook the remaining patties in the same manner.

Slice open the rolls, if using, and toast the bread or rolls. When toasted, spread the Tartar Sauce equally on each slice or the interiors of the rolls. Place 2 patties on each of 4 slices of bread or the bottom halves of the rolls. If necessary, slice and arrange the patties to fit the bread. Top the patties with the cucumber slices. Cover with the remaining slices of bread or the top halves of the rolls. Serve warm.

Chef's Tip: *For extra crunchiness, add some chopped celery to the just processed shrimp mixture.*

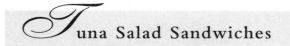

Tuna Salad Sandwiches

PANINI AL TONNO

Sometimes the best things are the simplest. Here's a version of this popular sandwich with a personal twist.

MAKES 4 HERO OR 6
STANDARD SANDWICHES

1 cup chopped cherry tomatoes (quarter them, then halve the quarters)

¼ teaspoon salt

½ cup mayonnaise

2 tablespoons tomato ketchup

1 tablespoon sweet pickle relish

2 6-ounce cans tuna packed in olive oil, drained

¼ cup finely diced onion

½ cup finely diced celery

2 tablespoons chopped pimiento-stuffed green olives

2 tablespoons tiny drained capers

3 tablespoons freshly grated Parmesan cheese

2 tablespoons chopped fresh mint

4 large, soft hero rolls, split, or 12 slices hearty country bread

1 whole clove garlic, peeled

Put the cherry tomatoes in a small bowl and sprinkle with the salt. In a separate bowl, combine the mayonnaise, ketchup, and relish well.

Place the tuna in a large bowl and break it up with a fork. Add the onion, celery, olives, capers, and Parmesan. Add 5 to 6 tablespoons of the mayonnaise mixture, and combine with a fork until all the ingredients are well mixed.

Drain the cherry tomatoes and fold them gently into the tuna mixture along with the mint.

Toast the rolls or bread, and when toasted, gently rub the interiors of the rolls or each of the slices of bread with the garlic. Spread the remaining mayonnaise mixture equally on the bottom halves of the rolls or half the slices of bread. Top with equal portions of the tuna mixture. Cover with the top halves of the rolls or the remaining slices of bread and serve.

Prosciutto, Shrimp, and Country Cream Sandwiches

PANINI MARE E MONTI

As its Italian name indicates, this recipe unites a bit of the sea, mare, *and a little something from the mountains,* monti, *in a glorious combination that travels well.*

MAKES 6 SANDWICHES

½ pound small peeled cooked shrimp

4 ounces cream cheese

¼ cup drained capers

1 tablespoon snipped fresh chives

1 teaspoon anchovy paste (optional)

6 Egg Buns (page 174), or soft hero or hoagie rolls

2 large whole cloves garlic, peeled

6 leaves romaine lettuce

2 or 3 fresh tomatoes, thinly sliced

6 ounces prosciutto or ham, thinly sliced

1 ounce Parmesan cheese, shaved (optional)

Freshly ground black pepper to taste

Preheat the broiler.

Place the shrimp, cream cheese, capers, chives, and anchovy paste, if using, in the bowl of a food processor, and purée to a thick paste. Refrigerate until ready to use.

Slice the buns or rolls in half lengthwise and toast in the broiler until golden brown. When toasted, gently rub the interiors of the buns or rolls with the garlic. Spread the bottom half of each with an equal amount of the shrimp paste. Top with a piece of lettuce trimmed to fit and a few slices of tomato. Divide the prosciutto or ham equally among the sandwiches and top with the Parmesan, if desired, and black pepper to taste. Cover with the top halves of the buns or rolls and serve.

Veal Cutlet Sandwiches

PANINI CON LE COTOLETTE

My mother used to take these sandwiches along when we traveled. Every time I eat one, I remember our trips to my grandmother's, and some of the best picnic lunches I've ever had.

MAKES 4 SANDWICHES

¾ pound fresh ripe tomatoes (2 or 3 small)

1½ tablespoon extra-virgin olive oil

¾ teaspoon plus 1 pinch coarse salt

3 tablespoons shredded fresh basil leaves

1 large clove garlic, finely minced

2 ounces mascarpone or cream cheese, softened

1 ounce fresh ricotta cheese

4 tablespoons freshly grated Parmesan cheese

1 cup Italian-Style Bread Crumbs (page 220)

2 tablespoons freshly grated Romano cheese

¼ teaspoon plus 1 pinch fresh ground black pepper

1 teaspoon paprika

½ cup all-purpose flour

2 eggs

¾ pound very thin veal scaloppine, cut into 8 equal portions (see Chef's Tip)

5 tablespoons olive oil

4 kaiser rolls, oversized hamburger buns, or other soft rolls

1 whole clove garlic, peeled

Core the tomatoes and cut them in half horizontally. Squeeze the halves gently or use a spoon to remove the seeds and pulp. Cut the squeezed tomatoes into ½-inch dice and place in a medium glass bowl. Add the olive oil, ¼ teaspoon of the salt, the basil and garlic. Toss well and set aside. (The tomatoes will let out additional liquid; this is what you want.)

In the bowl of a food processor, combine the mascarpone or cream cheese, ricotta, and Parmesan. Process until smooth, scraping down the sides of the bowl if necessary. Scrape the mixture into another bowl and set aside.

On a pie plate or large plate, combine the bread crumbs, Romano, ½ teaspoon of the salt, ¼ teaspoon of the pepper, and the paprika. On a second plate combine the flour with the pinch each of salt and pepper.

Beat the eggs in a small bowl. Dip a piece of veal into the eggs. Lift it out and let it drain. Dip it into the flour, coating both sides. Shake off the excess flour. Return it to the eggs, and let it drain again. Place it in the bread crumb mixture, spooning the crumbs over the veal and patting well to coat both sides. Place the breaded cutlet on a clean plate, and repeat the coating process with the remaining cutlets.

In a large, deep sauté pan, heat 3 tablespoons of the oil over medium-high heat. Add half the breaded cutlets to the hot oil and fry until dark golden brown, crispy, and cooked through, about 1 to 3 minutes on each side. Transfer to paper towels to drain. Add the remaining oil, fry the remaining cutlets, and transfer to paper towels when done.

Slice the rolls in half and toast them. Rub the interiors of the toasted rolls gently with the garlic. Spread a fourth of the cheese mixture on the bottom half of each roll. Place two cutlets on top, overlapping the pieces to fit the bread. Top with a few spoons of the tomato mixture, and drizzle a bit of the tomato liquid on the interior of the top half of each roll. Cover the sandwiches and serve.

Chef's Tip: *The veal I use is sliced very thin, so even 2 scaloppine per sandwich is fine. Have your butcher slice it very thin, or look for very thin cuts at your grocer's.*

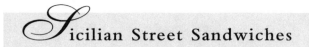

Sicilian Street Sandwiches

PANE E PANELLE

*You can still find street vendors making and selling these sandwiches in
Palermo. As a schoolboy, I ate one almost every day. Today I wonder how
I did it.*

MAKES 8 SANDWICHES

4 cups cold water

3 cups chickpea flour (available at specialty
 shops and health food stores)

2 teaspoons salt, plus additional for sprinkling

1 teaspoon freshly ground black pepper

Olive oil for greasing

2 pounds potatoes, peeled, boiled, and mashed
 (2½ cups)

1 cup freshly grated Parmesan cheese

1 whole egg plus 1 yolk

2 tablespoons chopped fresh Italian parsley

Extralight olive oil for frying

½ cup Italian-Style Bread Crumbs (page 220)

1 recipe Sicilian Buns (page 176), shaped into
 5-inch round rolls

In a medium saucepan, stir together the
water, chickpea flour, 1 teaspoon of the
salt, and ½ teaspoon of the pepper. Bring
the mixture to a boil over medium-high
heat, stirring often to prevent lumps from
forming. Cook until the mixture is very
thick and starts pulling away from the sides
of the pan, 15 to 20 minutes. A wooden
spoon should stand straight up by itself in
the mixture when it is finished.

Spread the hot chickpea dough on a
lightly oiled wooden cutting board or baking sheet, and let cool to room temperature. Cut the cooled dough into 2-inch
squares; you should have between 24 and
32 total. (These can be kept in an airtight
container in the refrigerator for up to a
week.)

In a large bowl, combine the potatoes,
Parmesan, egg and yolk, parsley, 1 teaspoon of the salt, and the remaining

pepper. Dampen your hands with water and shape the mixture into 16 oval croquettes, 1 x 3 inches each.

Heat at least 1 inch of the extralight oil to 375° in a wide, deep-sided sauté pan over medium-high heat. Fry the chickpea squares in the hot oil, a few at a time until they are brown, crisp, and puffy, about 2 minutes. Drain on paper towels and sprinkle with salt.

Place the bread crumbs in a pie plate or large plate, and roll the croquettes in the bread crumbs. Add extralight oil to the pan if needed, heat, and fry the croquettes, a few at a time, in the hot oil until golden brown and heated through, 2 to 3 minutes. Drain well on paper towels.

Slice the buns in half, place 3 or 4 chickpea fritters and 2 potato croquettes in each, and serve.

Mille Grazie

"Nicolino, telephone!" I heard my mother from the next room. Nanci and I had been in Palermo only a few days, and I was jet-lagged. Friends and family were calling at all hours.

"Who is it, Mamma?" I was not quite ready at that early hour to field telephone calls and answer dinner invitations. I walked into the room, and she held the receiver toward me.

"It's the mayor's office." She beamed at me with a mischievous grin.

This had to be my longtime friend Fabio, a practical joker who hasn't changed in all the years I've known him. Now he was impersonating someone from the mayor's office.

"Hello," I said in the most serious voice I could muster, which wasn't much: I could hardly stifle my laughter.

"Hello, Mr. Stellino, this is the press secretary at the mayor's office," a man's voice replied. "Our mayor, Leoluca Orlando, on behalf of the city of Palermo, would like to present you with a medal for what you've done to promote the Sicilian culinary tradition in America. The ceremony will be held at—"

I cut him off right there.

"Fabio," I said, "every year it's the same thing. So this time you're the mayor's office, eh? The older you get, the more creative you get. I'll tell you what, I'll swing by your house this afternoon with Nanci. Okay?" I hung up.

"Are you sure that was Fabio?" my mother asked. "It didn't sound like his voice."

Moments later the phone rang again.

"Mr. Stellino, please don't hang up, this isn't a joke. Our mayor would like you to be his guest at Villa Niscemi for a ceremony in which you will be presented with a medal from the city of Palermo. . . ."

The man went on, but I wasn't listening anymore. For once in my life I was speechless. Finally he ceased talking, and after a brief silence, I sputtered out a promise to be at Villa Niscemi with my family at four in the afternoon the next day. I hung up and turned to my mother, who simply nodded. She must have already decided what she would be wearing to the reception.

I had been to the villa about twenty years before, but not as an invited guest. At that time, the building was unoccupied and in the process of being restored. One day as I was driving by, I stopped outside it on a whim. I am a great admirer of Sicilian baroque villas and had read about this one; it was always cited as a masterly example of that architectural style. I slipped in through the front gate, but once inside the grounds I was stopped by a sleepy security guard, a large man with a warm smile, who introduced himself as Nunzio. Instead of ejecting me from the property, he led me on a tour of the formal rooms.

Even though the villa was in disrepair, it was beautiful. The main receiving hall was a long, high-ceilinged room adorned with splendid frescoes. Through the tall windows, I could see expansive terraces and the surrounding park. Other rooms were equally splendid, decorated with damask wall coverings and more frescoes. We emerged from the villa into the porte cochere, which, I supposed, was large enough to accommodate a carriage and four horses.

Now, twenty years after my first, unofficial visit to

the villa, as my mother, Nanci, and I headed toward the magnificent building, I remembered Nunzio's face. He would have laughed to know that his uninvited guest was back, this time by exclusive invitation, and about to be honored. The front gate was guarded by two tall Carabinieri in full ceremonial garb. Only the mayor and his police escort would be allowed to drive through the gate.

We entered the courtyard, where people were congregating: well-coifed ladies in their Sunday best, men stiff and warm in their suits, children eager to run but held in check by their watchful parents. By four o'clock, the place was full. There was a murmur in the crowd, and I could see a determined group of people striding across the courtyard, led by one of the Carabinieri who had been guarding the main entrance. Obviously this was the mayor and his party. They made their way into the villa, and we followed with the rest of the crowd.

Inside, in the cool of that large reception room that I remembered from younger days, I identified myself to a clerk seated by the door. I was quickly separated from my family and ushered onto a low stage at the far end of the room, where I joined a few others being honored with me. I was barely seated when the ceremony began. After a brief welcoming speech and introduction, Leoluca Orlando bustled up to the microphone. I expected to be sitting through a long-winded politician's talk and was hoping to come up with some witty remarks in case I spoke with him later. I searched the crowd for my family, but before I could locate them, I heard my name spoken loudly. I leaped to my feet and stepped toward the mayor, who grabbed my hand with a vigorous shake. Then he turned back to the assembly. I knew he must have been talking about me, but I wasn't really listening. I was looking for my mother. When I spotted her radiant face, I felt like a little boy in his first school play. The mayor placed a medal in my hand and guided me toward the microphone.

I don't recall exactly what I said. I hope that I expressed suitable gratitude for this great honor. If not, I would now like to offer this book as thanks to the mayor and the people of Palermo. It is a wonderful thing to be honored for doing what you love. But it is really generations of Italians who have pursued a passion for good food and love of life who deserve to be remembered and recognized.

Vi ringrazio con tutto il cuore.

Basics

This last section features mainly stocks, sauces, and spreads that are used with other recipes in the book. All of them, however, can be used in a wide variety of other dishes. Each of the pasta sauces, for example, can accompany any type of pasta, be it fresh, dry, or stuffed. And you might try the spreads—and some of the sauces—to liven up everyday sandwiches.

A word on stock: While homemade stock is superior to canned, I confess that, when pressed, I use commercially prepared products. If you use canned stock, however, I suggest you choose a reduced-sodium variety.

*I*talian-Style Bread Crumbs

PANE GRATTUGIATO

MAKES 1 1/2 CUPS

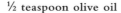

½ teaspoon olive oil

1 cup bread crumbs

1 tablespoon finely chopped fresh basil,
    or 1 teaspoon dried

1 tablespoon finely chopped fresh Italian
    parsley

⅛ teaspoon salt

⅛ teaspoon freshly ground black pepper

2 tablespoons freshly grated Romano or
    Parmesan cheese

In a nonstick sauté pan, heat the olive oil over medium heat for 1 minute. Add the bread crumbs and cook, stirring, until brown, about 2 minutes.

Transfer to a bowl, add the remaining ingredients, and mix well. Store in an airtight container or self-sealing plastic bag. Bread crumbs can be frozen for up to 2 months.

Beef Stock

BRODO DI MANZO

This is one member, with chicken stock and tomato sauce, of the trium-
virate of basics all chefs must master. You'll need two days to prepare it.

MAKES 2 1/4 QUARTS

5 tablespoons tomato paste

2 tablespoons all-purpose flour

6 pounds beef or veal bones

3 tablespoons olive oil

3 carrots, peeled and quartered

3 stalks celery, quartered

2 white onions, peeled and quartered

2 tablespoons chopped fresh rosemary,
   or 1½ teaspoons dried

1½ teaspoons dried thyme

2 tablespoons chopped fresh basil,
   or 1½ teaspoons dried

2 tablespoons chopped fresh Italian parsley,
   or 1½ teaspoons dried

1¼ tablespoons black peppercorns

3 bay leaves

4 whole cloves

¾ tablespoon salt

1¼ gallons water

4 egg whites (see Chef's Tip)

Preheat oven to 400°.

Mix the tomato paste and flour. Rub half of the mixture over the bones. Combine the oil and the rest of the tomato paste mixture with the carrots, celery, and onions in a bowl. Place the bones in a large roasting pan and bake until well browned, 20 to 30 minutes, turning them once. Be careful they do not burn. Place the vegetables in a second roasting pan and cook them on a rack below the bones for the same amount of time, turning once.

When they are done, transfer the bones and vegetables to a large stockpot, or two if you don't have one big enough; do not transfer the fat that has rendered at the bottom of the pan with the bones. Add the rest of the ingredients, except the egg whites, and bring the liquid to a boil. Reduce the heat and simmer the stock for 8 hours, skimming the foam that rises to

continued

the top every 30 minutes. Watch the pot, and as the stock reduces, add water as necessary to keep the bones just covered.

Discard the bones and strain the stock through a fine sieve lined with cheese-cloth. Let cool to room temperature and then place, uncovered, in the refrigera-tor overnight. The fat will harden and float to the top. Skim it off the next day and discard.

Bring the stock back to a boil. Beat the egg whites with a whisk or an electric beater until fluffy. Add to the boiling stock, reduce the heat to a simmer, and stir well. The egg whites will harden and trap most of the impurities. Strain the stock as before. You can use the stock at once, or freeze it for up to a month.

Chef's Tip: *Adding the egg whites will yield a clearer and more flavorful stock. If you don't mind a cloudy stock, you can omit them.*

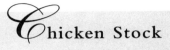

Chicken Stock

BRODO DI POLLO

This may take overnight, but once you taste it you'll think twice about using canned stock.

MAKES 2 1/4 QUARTS

3 to 3½ pounds chicken, cut in pieces

3 carrots, peeled and quartered

3 stalks celery, quartered

2 white onions, peeled and quartered

2 tablespoons chopped fresh rosemary, or 1½ teaspoons dried

1½ teaspoons dried thyme

2 tablespoons chopped fresh basil, or 1½ teaspoons dried

2 tablespoons chopped fresh Italian parsley, or 1½ teaspoons dried

1¼ tablespoons black peppercorns

¾ tablespoon salt

1½ cups white wine

3½ cups water

3 egg yolks, beaten

3 egg whites (see Chef's Tips)

Place all the ingredients except the egg whites in a large stockpot, bring the liquid to a boil, reduce the heat, and simmer for 2½ hours, skimming the foam that rises to the top every 30 minutes.

Remove the chicken and set aside for use in another recipe (see Chef's Tips). Strain the stock through a fine sieve lined with cheesecloth. Let cool to room temperature and then place, uncovered, in the refrigerator overnight. The fat will harden and float to the top. Skim it off the next day, and discard it.

Bring the stock back to a boil. Beat the egg whites with a whisk or an electric beater until fluffy. Add to the boiling stock, reduce the heat to a simmer, and stir well. The egg whites will harden and trap most of the impurities. Strain the stock as before. You can use the stock right away, or freeze it for up to one month.

continued

BASICS

Chef's Tips: *The egg whites will yield a clearer and more flavorful stock. If you don't mind a cloudy stock, you can omit them.*

Here's an idea for the leftover chicken: Chop the meat roughly, mix it with 1 or 2 beaten eggs, ½ cup freshly grated Parmesan cheese, and ½ cup Italian-Style Bread Crumbs. Shape the mixture into balls, and cook in the boiling stock before you add the egg whites. Serve the dumplings in your favorite soup. They can be frozen for up to 2 months.

ℳeat Sauce

RAGÙ DI CARNE

Classic ragù sauce originates in the Emilia-Romagna region, but versions of it are found throughout Italy.

MAKES 6 TO 7 CUPS

5 tablespoons olive oil

1 stalk celery, chopped

1 medium carrot, chopped

1 medium onion, chopped

6 cloves garlic, thickly sliced

¼ cup chopped fresh basil

2 tablespoons chopped fresh Italian parsley

1 tablespoon chopped fresh sage,
　　or 1 teaspoon dried

1 bay leaf

¼ teaspoon red pepper flakes

½ pound ground veal

½ pound ground lamb

½ pound ground beef

2 ounces prosciutto or ham, diced

1 cup red wine

3 cups Tomato Sauce (page 229)

½ cup tomato paste

1 cup Beef Stock (page 221) or Chicken Stock
　　(page 223)

1 teaspoon salt

½ teaspoon freshly ground black pepper

In a large pot, heat the oil over medium heat. Add the celery, carrot, onion, and garlic, and sauté slowly, until tender and sweet, 6 to 8 minutes. (For a smoother sauce, pulse the celery, whole carrot, and onion in a food processor for less than a minute to a rough paste before sautéing.) Stir in the basil, parsley, sage, bay leaf, and red pepper flakes. Increase the heat to medium-high and add the veal, lamb, beef, and prosciutto or ham. Cook, stirring often, until the meats start to brown, 6 to 8 minutes. Add the wine, gently scraping the pan to dislodge any browned bits from the bottom. Simmer until the wine is reduced by half, about 3 minutes.

Mix in the Tomato Sauce, tomato paste, stock, salt, and pepper. Bring the mixture to a boil, reduce the heat, and simmer, covered, for 45 minutes, stirring occasionally. For a thicker sauce, remove the lid after 30 minutes and simmer, uncovered, until rich and concentrated.

White Meat Sauce

RAGÙ IN BIANCO

If the idea of a white meat sauce seems strange, let me assure you that this tastes great.

MAKES 4 CUPS

5 tablespoons olive oil

1 stalk celery, chopped

1 medium carrot, chopped

1 medium onion, chopped

6 cloves garlic, thickly sliced

¼ cup chopped fresh basil

2 tablespoons chopped fresh Italian parsley

1 tablespoon chopped fresh sage,
    or 1 teaspoon dried

1 bay leaf

¼ teaspoon red pepper flakes

1½ pounds ground veal (see Chef's Tip)

2 ounces prosciutto or ham, diced

1 cup white wine

2 cups Chicken Stock (page 223)

1 teaspoon salt

½ teaspoon freshly ground black pepper

In a large saucepan, heat the oil over medium heat. Add the celery, carrot, onion, and garlic, and sauté slowly until tender, 6 to 8 minutes. (For a smoother sauce, pulse the celery, whole carrot, and onion in a food processor for less than a minute to a rough paste before sautéing.) Stir in the basil, parsley, sage, bay leaf, and red pepper flakes. Increase the heat to medium-high and add the veal and prosciutto or ham. Cook, stirring often, until the meats start to brown, 10 to 12 minutes.

Add the wine, gently scraping the pan to dislodge any browned bits from the bottom. Simmer until the liquid is reduced by half, about 3 minutes. Add the stock and season with the salt and pepper. Bring the liquid to a boil, reduce the heat, and simmer, uncovered, for 45 minutes, until the sauce is thick and rich.

Chef's Tip: *You may substitute ground turkey or chicken for veal.*

BASICS

Rustic Lamb Sauce

RAGÙ DI AGNELLO ALLA RUSTICA

Try this on any kind of pasta, and enjoy its explosive flavor. The long marinating time will be worth it.

MAKES 4 CUPS

1½ pounds lamb shoulder or sirloin

1 cup diced carrot

1 cup diced onion

1 cup diced celery

10 large cloves garlic, thickly sliced

1 sprig fresh rosemary

1 bay leaf

2 tablespoons olive oil

1 cup red wine

1 14.5-ounce can Italian-style whole peeled tomatoes, drained and chopped

½ teaspoon salt

½ teaspoon freshly ground black pepper

In a medium bowl or casserole, combine the lamb, carrot, onion, celery, garlic, rosemary, and bay leaf. Marinate in the refrigerator at least 8 hours, possibly overnight.

Strain the liquid from the meat and vegetables, and set aside. Remove the meat and pat dry. Reserve the vegetables.

Heat the oil in a medium sauté pan or casserole over medium heat. Add the meat and brown evenly on all sides, 3 to 4 minutes per side. Remove the meat from the pan and keep warm. Add the reserved vegetables to the same pan and sauté until tender, 8 to 10 minutes. Increase the heat to medium-high and add reserved marinating liquid, stirring to dislodge any browned bits from the bottom of the pan. Simmer until liquid is reduced by half, 5 to 6 minutes.

Return the meat to the pan and add the tomatoes, salt, and pepper. Bring the liquid to a boil, cover, and reduce the heat. Simmer, covered, for 2½ hours, until the meat is extremely tender. Break up and shred the meat with two forks, and remove any bones. Stir the meat into the sauce. Continue to cook over medium-low heat for 20 minutes, stirring well to incorporate the flavors.

Tomato Sauce

SUGO DI POMODORO

In a pinch you can always use your favorite store-bought tomato sauce, but nothing tastes better than homemade. When you have the time, give this recipe a try; you will be impressed.

MAKES 7 1/2 CUPS

6 tablespoons olive oil

6 whole cloves garlic, peeled

1¼ cups chopped onion

1½ teaspoons red pepper flakes

3 28-ounce cans Italian-style whole peeled tomatoes, drained and chopped, juice reserved

½ teaspoon salt

½ teaspoon freshly ground black pepper

1 teaspoon sugar (optional)

8 tablespoon chopped fresh basil, or 2½ teaspoons dried

½ teaspoon dried oregano

Heat the oil in a 3-quart stockpot over medium-high heat. Add the garlic, onion, and red pepper flakes, and cook over medium heat, stirring often, for 15 minutes, until the onion starts to brown. Add the remaining ingredients (use the sugar only if the tomatoes are not sweet enough for you), and cook, stirring well, for 5 minutes.

Add the reserved tomato juice, bring to a boil, reduce the heat, and simmer for 30 to 35 minutes, stirring occasionally. Use the sauce right away, or let cool to room temperature and store for later use: refrigerated for up to 3 days, or frozen for up to 1 month.

Chef's Tip: *For a smoother, more elegant presentation, cool the sauce to room temperature and process it, in batches, in a food processor. The color may change slightly, but the flavor will remain outstanding.*

*S*picy Tomato Sauce

SUGO DI POMODORO PICCANTE

Here's a tomato sauce with a kick.

MAKES 2 1/4 CUPS

2 cups Tomato Sauce (page 229)

2 cups Chicken Stock (page 223)

¼ cup chopped fresh Italian parsley

6 large cloves garlic, thickly sliced

¼ teaspoon red pepper flakes

1 teaspoon cold unsalted butter (optional)

In a medium saucepan, combine all the ingredients except the butter, and simmer over medium heat until the mixture reaches a sauce consistency, 10 to 12 minutes. Purée the sauce in a blender or food processor, with the butter if desired, to add a shine.

Tomato Sauce Mantua Style

SUGO MANTOVANO

I love the full-bodied flavor of this sauce, which I first tried in Mantua.

MAKES 2 1/2 CUPS

2 cups Tomato Sauce (page 229)

2 cups Beef Stock (page 221)

Half a smoked ham hock, or a prosciutto bone
(10 to 12 ounces)

Place all the ingredients in a medium saucepan and bring the liquid to a boil. Reduce the heat and simmer for 45 minutes to 1 hour, until the sauce is reduced to about 2½ cups. Remove any meat remaining on the bone and stir it into the sauce. Discard the bone.

Creamed Tomato-Caper Sauce

CREMA DI POMODORO E CAPPERI

This tomato sauce is a great accompaniment to grilled fish.

MAKES 2 CUPS

1½ cups Tomato Sauce (page 229)

¾ cup Chicken Stock (page 223)

3 tablespoons chopped fresh Italian parsley

3 tablespoons unsalted butter

3 tablespoons drained and rinsed capers

⅛ teaspoon salt

⅛ teaspoon freshly ground black pepper

Pinch sugar

Combine the sauce, stock, and 2 tablespoons of the parsley in a blender or food processor and process to a smooth, velvety texture. Transfer the mixture to a medium saucepan and bring to a boil. Add the remaining parsley, remove the pan from the heat, and whisk in the butter 1 tablespoon at a time until it just melts into the sauce. Stir in the capers and season with the salt, pepper, and sugar. Reheat gently without letting the sauce boil.

Chef's Tip: *If you make this a little ahead of time (no more than 2 to 3 hours before using), keep it warm in a double boiler.*

Passione

232

Pizza Sauce

SUGO PER LA PIZZA

You can expand this very basic recipe to your own liking.

MAKES 2 1/4 CUPS

1¾ cups Tomato Sauce (page 229),
    or 1 15-ounce can tomato sauce

½ cup tomato paste

2 teaspoons sugar

½ teaspoon garlic powder

¼ teaspoon dried oregano

Combine the ingredients in a blender or food processor and blend until smooth, about 20 seconds.

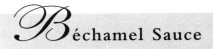

Béchamel Sauce

BESCIAMELLA

Here is a basic of the cucina italiana, *simple to make and an elegant touch in any dish.*

MAKES ABOUT 2 CUPS

3 tablespoons unsalted butter

2 tablespoons all-purpose flour

2 cups whole milk

¼ teaspoon salt, plus additional to taste

¼ teaspoon freshly ground black pepper, plus additional to taste

1 bay leaf

¼ teaspoon freshly grated nutmeg

Melt the butter in a medium saucepan. Sprinkle in the flour, and stir with a wooden spoon until well blended. Cook, stirring, for 2 to 3 minutes, until the mixture is a golden brown. Remove this thin paste, or roux, from the heat.

In another medium saucepan, heat the milk, ¼ teaspoon each salt and pepper, bay leaf, and nutmeg until the milk is steaming. Remove the bay leaf.

Return the roux to the heat, and slowly pour in the steaming milk mixture, whisking constantly to prevent lumps. Continue stirring over medium heat for 3 to 6 minutes. When the mixture thickens, remove from the heat and season with salt and pepper to taste.

Chef's Tips: *To make in advance, dot the surface of the finished sauce with additional butter or place a piece of buttered waxed paper directly on it to prevent a skin from forming. Reheat gently as needed, without letting the sauce cook.*

You might also try these interesting variations:

For Parmesan Béchamel Sauce, add 1 cup freshly grated Parmesan cheese after removing the thickened roux-milk mixture from the heat. Allow the cheese to melt, and then season with the salt and pepper to taste. This goes well with any type of baked pasta.

For Basil Parmesan Béchamel Sauce, add ¼ cup very thinly sliced fresh basil along with the 1 cup freshly grated Parmesan cheese as described above.

$\mathcal{C}$urry Sauce

SALSA AL CURRY

This delectable sauce is a perfect partner for the shellfish of your choice.

MAKES 2 1/2 CUPS

2½ cups whole milk

1 tablespoon curry powder

½ teaspoon salt

¼ teaspoon freshly ground black pepper

¼ teaspoon freshly grated nutmeg

3 tablespoons unsalted butter

2 tablespoons all-purpose flour

Combine the milk, curry powder, salt, pepper, and nutmeg in a medium saucepan. Cook slowly until the milk is steaming, and set aside. In another medium saucepan, melt the butter and stir in the flour with a wooden spoon. Cook this thin paste, or roux, over medium heat for 2 minutes, until golden.

Pour the hot milk mixture into the warm roux, stirring constantly. Cook the sauce over medium heat until it just thickens, about 3 to 5 minutes. Remove from the heat.

Chef's Tip: *If you are not using the béchamel immediately, dot the surface of the finished sauce with additional butter or place a piece of buttered waxed paper directly on the surface to prevent a skin from forming. Reheat gently as needed, without letting the sauce cook.*

Garlic Cream Sauce

CREMA ALL'AGLIO

Garlic lovers, here is the sauce of your dreams. Use it on any pasta dish.

MAKES 1 1/2 CUPS

2 cups heavy cream

6 large cloves garlic, thickly sliced

⅛ teaspoon salt

⅛ teaspoon freshly ground black pepper

Combine the ingredients in a medium saucepan, and simmer for 15 to 20 minutes, until the sauce is thick enough to coat the back of a spoon.

STELLINO

BASICS

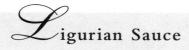

Ligurian Sauce

SALSA LIGURE

This recipe is ideal for summertime pasta salads.

MAKES ABOUT 2 CUPS

2 or 3 thick slices day-old bread, crusts removed

½ cup heavy cream

1 10-ounce box frozen chopped spinach, thawed, or 1 large bunch fresh spinach, blanched and chopped

½ cup pine nuts

¼ cup sun-dried tomatoes (6 or 7 halves) packed in olive oil, drained and chopped

4 large cloves garlic, minced

¼ cup freshly grated Parmesan cheese

¼ teaspoon salt

¼ teaspoon freshly ground black pepper

1 cup extra-virgin olive oil

Soak the bread in the cream until it is completely soft, about 1 hour. Squeeze the bread dry. Squeeze as much moisture as possible out of the spinach.

In a food processor, pulse the spinach, pine nuts, sun-dried tomatoes, and garlic until well blended. Add the softened bread, Parmesan, salt, and pepper, and purée to a thick paste. With the processor on, add the oil in a thin stream to make a thick, emulsified sauce.

Piedmontese Sauce

SUGO PIEMONTESE

This very rich sauce, suitable for any type of pasta, goes well with a full-bodied red wine.

MAKES 3 TO 3 1/2 CUPS

4 tablespoons olive oil

8 ounces Italian-style sausage, casing removed

6 large cloves garlic, thickly sliced

1 cup chopped onion

2 ounces prosciutto or ham, chopped

4 ounces salami, chopped

½ cup red wine

1½ cups Beef Stock (page 221)

½ cup heavy cream

½ teaspoon freshly ground black pepper

Heat the oil over medium-high heat in a skillet or sauté pan. Add the sausage and brown it, breaking up the meat with a wooden spoon as it cooks, about 5 to 6 minutes. Remove from the pan with a slotted spoon and set aside. Drain the pan of all but 2 to 3 tablespoons of the fat in the bottom.

In the same pan, cook the garlic and onion until the garlic starts to brown and the onion becomes translucent, 2 to 3 minutes. Add the prosciutto or ham, salami, and sausage, and then the wine, stirring to dislodge any browned bits from the bottom of the pan. Simmer to reduce the liquid by half, about 2 minutes. Add the stock, cream, and pepper, and bring the liquid to a boil. Reduce the heat and simmer 12 to 15 minutes to a sauce consistency.

arma Sauce

SUGO ALLA PARMIGIANA

When I first had this sauce, in a small trattoria in Parma, it was served with pumpkin ravioli. You can pair it with whatever type of pasta you like.

MAKES 1 1/2 TO 2 CUPS

2 tablespoons unsalted butter

4 large cloves garlic, thickly sliced

4 ounces prosciutto or ham, chopped

⅛ teaspoon red pepper flakes

½ cup sparkling white wine

1 tablespoon tomato paste (optional)

1 cup heavy cream

¼ teaspoon freshly ground black pepper

Melt the butter in a skillet or sauté pan over medium-high heat. Add the garlic, prosciutto or ham, and red pepper flakes, and sauté until the garlic is golden brown, 1 to 2 minutes. Add the wine, and stir to dislodge any browned bits from the bottom of the pan. Simmer to reduce the wine by half, 1 to 2 minutes. Stir in the tomato paste, if desired, until the mixture is smooth. Add the cream and pepper, and bring the mixture to a boil. Reduce the heat and simmer to a sauce consistency, 10 to 12 minutes.

Passione

Turkey and Bell Pepper Sauce

PEPERONATA AL TACCHINO

The turkey and the bell pepper are a rustic yet elegant mix. This sauce is a good choice with any pasta.

MAKES 3 TO 3 1/2 CUPS

3 tablespoons olive oil

6 large cloves garlic, thickly sliced, then roughly chopped

½ teaspoon red pepper flakes

¾ cup finely diced onion

¾ cup finely diced carrot

1½ cups diced red bell pepper

1 pound ground turkey

1 teaspoon salt

½ teaspoon freshly ground black pepper

¾ cup Marsala wine

1 tablespoon chopped fresh Italian parsley

1 tablespoon chopped fresh thyme

1 tablespoon chopped fresh tarragon

1½ cups Tomato Sauce (page 229)

1½ cups Chicken Stock (page 223)

½ cup heavy cream

In a large, deep sauté pan, heat the oil over medium-high heat. Add the garlic, red pepper flakes, onion, carrot, and bell pepper. Sauté until the vegetables are soft, about 5 minutes.

Increase the heat slightly, and add the turkey, salt, and black pepper. Sauté, breaking the turkey apart with a wooden spoon, until the meat is just cooked through, about 2 to 3 minutes. Add the Marsala, stir well, and cook until the liquid is reduced by half, about 1 to 2 minutes. Stir in the parsley, thyme, and tarragon.

Add the Tomato Sauce and stock. Bring to a boil, reduce the heat, and simmer for about 20 minutes. Add the cream, stir, and simmer until the mixture thickens to a sauce consistency, 5 to 10 minutes.

Chef's Tip: *Ground chicken works just as well as turkey in this recipe, so you might substitute it in the sauce. Dark meat is moister— and even better—than white meat.*

Calabrian Sauce with Sausage

SUGO DI SALSICCIA ALLA CALABRESE

The robust flavors of this hearty sauce go well with any type of pasta and a fine glass of red wine.

MAKES 2 1/2 TO 3 CUPS

2 tablespoons olive oil

8 cloves garlic, thickly sliced

¾ cup finely chopped onion

½ teaspoon red pepper flakes

8 ounces sweet Italian-style sausage, casing removed

1 28-ounce can Italian-style whole peeled tomatoes, drained and coarsely chopped, juice reserved

½ cup red wine

Heat the oil in a large, deep sauté pan over medium-high heat. Add the garlic, onion, and red pepper flakes, and sauté for 2 to 3 minutes. Add the sausage, breaking it up into fine pieces with a wooden spoon. Stir the mixture and cook for 3 to 4 more minutes, until the sausage is browned and cooked through. Add the tomatoes, stir the mixture well, and cook until the liquid from the tomatoes absorbed, about 5 to 7 minutes.

Add the wine, stirring to dislodge any browned bits from the bottom of the pan. Cook over medium-high heat until the liquid has reduced by half, about 2 to 3 minutes. Add 2 cups of the reserved tomato juice and stir well. Bring the liquid to a boil, reduce the heat, and cook at a low simmer until the mixture reaches a sauce consistency, 15 to 20 minutes.

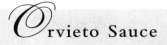rvieto Sauce

SUGO DI ORVIETO

The cathedral of Orvieto is not the town's only masterpiece, as this sauce will prove. I like the thick consistency and intense flavor, which complement any type of pasta.

MAKES 2 1/2 TO 3 CUPS

¾ pound fresh asparagus

¾ pound cremini or white button mushrooms

4 tablespoons olive oil

¾ pound pancetta, cut into ¼-inch dice, or bacon, cut into small pieces

6 cloves garlic, thickly sliced

¼ packed cup chopped fresh Italian parsley

Scant ½ teaspoon red pepper flakes

½ cup brandy

2 cups Chicken Stock (page 223)

½ cup Tomato Sauce (page 229)

½ cup heavy cream

Snap or cut off the woody ends of the asparagus and discard. If the spears are thick, peel the lower parts with a vegetable peeler. Cut off the tips, and cut the remaining stalks into ½-inch pieces. Set aside tips and stalks. Cut the mushrooms in half vertically, and cut each half into ½-inch-thick slices. Set aside.

In a large, deep sauté pan, heat 2 tablespoons of the oil over medium-high heat. Add the pancetta or bacon, in two batches if necessary, and sauté until browned, 6 to 7 minutes. Remove with a slotted spoon, and set aside.

Add the remaining oil to the pan, and then the asparagus and garlic, and sauté over medium-high heat until the asparagus is browned but still firm, about 6 minutes. Remove the asparagus with a slotted spoon and set aside. Add the mushrooms,

continued

parsley, and red pepper flakes to the pan, and sauté over medium-high heat for 4 to 5 minutes, until the mushrooms are browned and beginning to soften.

Return the asparagus and pancetta or bacon to the pan, and stir well to combine the ingredients. Add the brandy and cook for 2 to 3 minutes. Add the stock, Tomato Sauce, and cream, and stir well. Bring the liquid to a boil, reduce the heat, and simmer until the mixture reaches a sauce consistency, about 30 minutes.

Arriminata Sauce

SALSA ARRIMINATA

One of my father's aunts used to make this sauce. She called it arriminata di carciofi, *or loosely, "artichoke mix-up." My father and I each have our own version. Mine includes sausage, to make it even more hearty.*

MAKES 3 TO 3 1/2 CUPS

Juice of 1 lemon

5 fresh artichokes (see Chef's Tip)

4 tablespoons olive oil

1 pound sweet Italian-style sausage, casing removed

6 cloves garlic, thickly sliced

½ teaspoon red pepper flakes

6 sun-dried tomato halves, packed in oil, thickly sliced

¼ packed cup chopped fresh Italian parsley

1 cup white wine

1½ cups Chicken Stock (page 223)

1½ cups Tomato Sauce (page 229)

Fill a bowl with cold water, and add the lemon juice. Trim the stem ends from the artichokes. Peel off the dark outer leaves until you reach the soft yellow ones. With a paring knife, trim to smooth the rough edges where the leaves were removed. Quarter the artichokes vertically. You will see the heart, the choke, and purple-topped leaves. Cut off the leaves. With a grapefruit spoon or a paring knife, follow the line where the hairy choke meets the heart and remove the choke. Cut each heart into ½-inch pieces and drop them immediately into the lemon water; do not drain them until right before using. You should have roughly 2 cups of pieces.

In a large, deep sauté pan, heat 2 table-spoons of the oil over medium-high heat. Add the sausage and sauté, breaking it up into very small pieces with a wooden

continued

spoon, until cooked through, about 5 to 7 minutes. Remove the sausage with a slotted spoon and set aside.

Add the remaining oil and heat for 1 minute; add the garlic, red pepper flakes, drained artichoke hearts, and sun-dried tomatoes. Sauté until the artichokes have browned and begin to soften, about 6 to 8 minutes. Add the parsley and sausage, and cook, stirring, 1 to 2 minutes. Add the wine, stirring to dislodge any browned bits from the bottom of the pan. Stir well and cook for 5 minutes.

Add the stock and Tomato Sauce, and stir well. Bring the liquid to a boil, reduce the heat, and simmer until the liquid reaches a sauce consistency, about 20 to 25 minutes.

Chef's Tip: *If you can't find fresh artichokes, substitute 2 cups thawed frozen artichoke hearts, or 2 cups rinsed and drained canned.*

Fontina and Asparagus Sauce

SUGO DI FONTINA E ASPARAGI

Fontina, the best of which comes from the Val d'Aosta region, is a superb cheese, on its own or in combination as here.

MAKES 1 1/2 TO 2 CUPS

1 pound fresh asparagus (thin stalks)

4 tablespoons olive oil

6 cloves garlic, thickly sliced

¼ teaspoon red pepper flakes

½ teaspoon salt

¼ teaspoon freshly ground black pepper

¼ cup white wine

½ cup Chicken Stock (page 223)

1 cup whole milk

2 egg yolks

4 ounces Fontina cheese, grated

¼ cup freshly grated Parmesan cheese

Bring a large pot of salted water to a boil.

Snap or cut off the woody ends of the asparagus and discard. Cut off the tips, and cut the remaining stalks into ½-inch pieces. Set aside tips and stalks.

Heat the oil in large, deep sauté pan over medium-high heat. Add the garlic and red pepper flakes, and sauté for 1 to 2 minutes. Add the asparagus, salt, and pepper, and sauté for 5 to 6 minutes. Add the wine, stirring to dislodge any browned bits from the bottom of the pan, and simmer until most of the liquid is gone, about 4 minutes. Add the stock and continue to cook over medium-high heat until most of the liquid is absorbed and the asparagus is cooked through, with a nice glaze, about 8 to 10 minutes. Turn off the heat.

Warm the milk in a double boiler, over simmering (not boiling) water. When the milk is warm to the touch, whisk in the

continued

egg yolks, one at a time, until thoroughly combined. Cook, stirring constantly, for 2 to 4 minutes. Stir in the cheeses, and continue stirring as they melt, for 1 to 2 minutes; be careful not to overheat or overcook the cheese mixture. Fold in the asparagus mixture and turn off the heat.

Chef's Tip: *If you don't use the sauce immediately, keep it warm in the double boiler, stirring occasionally to prevent a skin from forming on top.*

$\mathscr{P}$ea Sauce

SUGO DI PISELLI

Try this with meat or cheese tortellini.

1 10-ounce package frozen peas

1 cup Chicken Stock (page 223)

½ cup heavy cream

½ teaspoon salt

½ teaspoon freshly ground black pepper

In a medium saucepan, simmer the peas, stock, and cream until the peas are tender but still bright green, 4 to 5 minutes. Purée the mixture in a blender or food processor. Return to the pan and season with the salt and pepper. Simmer the sauce until it is just thick enough to coat the back of a spoon, 6 to 7 minutes.

BASICS

$\mathcal{Q}$uick Shrimp Sauce

SUGHETTO DI GAMBERI AL LAMPO

You'll think twice about automatically discarding shrimp shells once you've tried this delightful sauce.

MAKES ABOUT 2 CUPS

2 tablespoons olive oil

1 cup chopped onion

1 medium carrot, chopped

1 stalk celery, chopped

4 large cloves garlic, thickly sliced

Shells from ¾ pound medium shrimp
  (2 to 3 cups)

⅛ teaspoon red pepper flakes

½ cup white wine

1 cup clam juice or Chicken Stock (page 223)

1 cup Tomato Sauce (page 229)

¼ teaspoon salt

¼ teaspoon freshly ground black pepper

Heat the oil over medium heat in a large saucepan. Add the onion, carrot, celery, and garlic, and sauté until the onion is soft and aromatic but not brown, 5 to 6 minutes. Add the shrimp shells and red pepper flakes, and cook until the shells turn red, 2 to 3 minutes.

Add the wine, stirring gently to dislodge any browned bits from the bottom of the pan. Simmer and reduce the liquid by half, 1 to 2 minutes. Add the clam juice or stock, Tomato Sauce, salt, and pepper, and bring the liquid to a boil. Reduce the heat, and simmer until the sauce has thickened slightly, 8 to 10 minutes. Strain the sauce, pressing the shrimp shells softly with a wooden spoon to extract the flavor. Discard the solids and return the sauce to the pan to warm through.

Passione

$\mathcal{R}$oasted Garlic Sauce

SUGO ALL'AGLIO ARROSTITO

If you love garlic as much as I do, you will find a thousand uses for this sauce.

MAKES 2 1/2 CUPS

2 tablespoons olive oil

½ cup chopped onion

1 tablespoon chopped fresh Italian parsley

⅛ teaspoon red pepper flakes

2 tablespoons roasted garlic pulp
   (see Chef's Tip)

1 cup Tomato Sauce (page 229)

1 cup Chicken Stock (page 223)

½ cup heavy cream

½ teaspoon salt

½ teaspoon freshly ground black pepper

Heat the oil in a saucepan over medium heat. Add the onion, parsley, and red pepper flakes, and sauté until the onion is tender, 6 to 8 minutes. Add the garlic pulp and mix well. Stir in the Tomato Sauce, stock, cream, salt, and pepper. Bring the liquid to a boil, reduce the heat, and simmer until the mixture reaches a sauce consistency, 10 to 12 minutes.

Chef's Tip: *To make the pulp: Preheat the oven to 350°. Cut off the top of 3 heads of garlic to expose the cloves. Place the garlic, cut side up, in a small baking pan. Drizzle with 2 tablespoons olive oil and 2 tablespoons Chicken Stock, and season with a dried bay leaf and a pinch of salt and pepper. Cover the pan with foil and bake for 45 minutes, or until the garlic is soft and sweet. Cool slightly. Squeeze the roasted garlic from the heads, and mash the softened garlic in a bowl with a spoon or fork.*

BASICS

stica Sauce

SUGO DI USTICA

Sometimes you must improvise, and the results are better than you could ever have imagined. This recipe is an example of such luck.

MAKES 2 CUPS

3 tablespoons olive oil

4 ounces pancetta, cut into ¼-inch dice, or bacon, cut into small pieces

1 small onion, finely diced

6 cloves garlic, thickly sliced

¼ to ½ teaspoon red pepper flakes to taste

1 28-ounce can whole plum tomatoes, drained and chopped, juice reserved

½ teaspoon dried oregano

½ cup red wine

½ cup water

Salt and freshly ground black pepper to taste

¼ cup chopped fresh basil

Heat the oil in a large, deep sauté pan, over medium-high heat. Add the pancetta or bacon and sauté until it starts to brown, about 3 to 4 minutes. Add the onion, garlic, and red pepper flakes, and sauté for 5 to 6 minutes, until the onion is soft and translucent. Add the tomatoes and oregano, and sauté until the tomatoes begin to look dry, about 6 to 7 minutes.

Add the wine, stirring with a wooden spoon to dislodge any browned bits from the bottom of the pan. Cook, stirring, until the wine reduces by half, about 2 to 3 minutes. Add 1½ cups of the reserved tomato juice, the water, and salt and pepper to taste. Bring the liquid to a boil, reduce the heat, and simmer until the mixture reaches a sauce consistency, about 10 to 12 minutes. Stir in the basil, and the sauce is ready.

Caesar Sandwich Spread

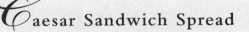

CONDIMENTO DI CESARE

Here's an imperial remedy for any sandwich in need of some zip.

MAKES 3/4 CUP

2 whole cloves garlic, peeled

2 anchovy fillets packed in oil, drained

3 tablespoons freshly squeezed lemon juice

2 teaspoons Dijon mustard

5 tablespoons freshly grated Parmesan cheese

3 dashes Tabasco or hot sauce

2 teaspoons balsamic vinegar

5 tablespoons olive oil

Place the garlic and anchovy fillets in the bowl of a food processor fitted with a metal blade, and process until finely chopped. Scrape down the sides of the bowl with a spatula. Add the lemon juice, mustard, Parmesan, Tabasco or hot sauce, and vinegar, and process until well combined. With the processor on, slowly drizzle in the oil. Pulse the mixture until well combined.

Chef's Tip: *This is a thick spread; leftovers will thicken even further in the refrigerator.*

Tartar Sauce

SALSA TARTARA

This recipe is too simple to resist.

MAKES 1/2 CUP

½ cup mayonnaise

2 tablespoons sweet pickle relish

1 heaping teaspoon chopped pimiento-stuffed green olives

1 heaping teaspoon drained tiny capers

1 teaspoon freshly squeezed lemon juice

Combine the ingredients in a bowl, and stir well.

Passione

*O*live-Caper Cream Cheese Spread

CREMA DI CAPPERI E OLIVE

Add this to your favorite sandwich for an extra kick.

MAKES 3/4 CUP

8 ounces mascarpone or cream cheese, softened

1 tablespoon balsamic vinegar

½ cup diced red bell pepper, cut into ¼-inch dice

2 tablespoons chopped pitted black olives

4 tablespoons drained tiny capers

2 tablespoons finely chopped fresh Italian parsley

Combine the ingredients in a bowl. Stir until well mixed; the spread should look like confetti cream cheese.

Chef's Tip: *For a saltier spread, substitute pimiento-stuffed green olives for the black, or use them in addition to the black.*

BASICS

Index

Accussì, 84–89, 97–98
American-Style Pepperoni Pizza, 149
anchovies
  Caesar Sandwich Spread, 253
  Neapolitan Pizza, 148
anchovy paste
  Pasta Boats, 26–27
  Sandwiches Tartare, 201
Arborio rice, 105
Arriminata Sauce, 245–46
  gnocchi with, 103
artichokes
  Arriminata Sauce, 245–46
    gnocchi with, 103
  pappardelle with prosciutto, truffle, and, 65–66
  Pizza Four Seasons, 150–51
  ravioli, 42–44
  stuffed pizza with prosciutto, three cheeses, and, 168–69
Asiago, 106
  Four-Cheese Pizza, 131
  Portobello Mushroom and Cheese Sandwiches, 196–97
asparagus
  and Fontina sauce, 247–48
    pappardelle with, 69
  Orvieto Sauce, 243–44
  and prosciutto sandwiches, 198–99
attitude in cooking, 1–2
authentic cuisine, 4

bacon. *See* pancetta
Barchette di Pasta, 26–27
basil
  and Parmesan Béchamel Sauce, 235
  Fried Calzones, 139–40
  Pizza Margherita, 152
beans, lima, in Prosciutto Sandwiches with Mint, Mascarpone, and Parmesan, 179
Béchamel Sauce, 234–35

beef
  ground, in Meat Sauce, 225
    fried pizza dumplings stuffed with, 141–42
  Sandwiches Tartare, 201
  stock, 221–22
beets, pasta with sauce of sausage, Gorgonzola, and, 28–29
Besciamella, 234–35
Black Squid Risotto, 110–11
bologna, 18
bread. *See* Egg Buns; flatbread; *panini*; sandwiches; Sicilian Buns
bread crumbs, Italian-style, 220
Bread Gnocchi with Tomato Sauce, 97–98
Brodo di Manzo, 221–22
Brodo di Pollo, 223–24
broth. *See* stock

Caesar Sandwich Spread, 253
  Chicken Caesar Sandwiches, 183–84
Calabrian Sauce with Sausage, 242
  ravioli with, 67–68
calzones (*calzoni*)
  baked, with prosciutto and mozzarella, 130
  fried, 139–40
Camembert
  sandwiches, prosciutto, pâté, and, 182
  stuffed pizza with radicchio, prosciutto, and, 170–71
Cannelloni Mantua Style, 45–46
capers
  -and-olive cream cheese spread, 255
  and salami sandwiches, 200
  Pasta Boats, 26–27
  pizza with olives, eggplant, and, 156–57
  Sandwiches Tartare, 201
  -and-tomato sauce, creamed, 232

tortellini with smoked salmon and, 79
  Tuna Salad Sandwiches, 208
carrots
  Pasta with Prosciutto-and-Vegetable Sauce, 19–20
  Vegetarian Lasagnette, 82–83
Cecina alla Lucchese, 136
celery, in Pasta with Prosciutto-and-Vegetable Sauce, 19–20
cheese
  Baked Pasta with Sausage and Zucchini, 13–14
  Braised-Pepper Pizza, 134–35
  Cannelloni Mantua Style, 45–46
  Four-Cheese Pizza, 131
  goat, pizza with sausage and, 160
  Gruyère. *See* Swiss
  Pasta Boats, 26–27
  and portobello mushroom sandwiches, 196–97
  Ravioli with Calabrian Sauce with Sausage, 67–68
  for risotto, 106
  stuffed pizza with prosciutto, artichokes, and, 168–69
  Swiss, Fried Calzones, 139–40
  See also Asiago; Camembert; cream cheese; Fontina; Gorgonzola; mascarpone; mozzarella; Parmesan; pecorino; provolone; ricotta; Romano
chicken
  Caesar sandwiches, 183–84
  salad sandwiches, 187–88
  stock, 223–24
Chickpea Pizza Lucca Style, 136
clams
  pasta with pancetta, mushrooms, and, 30–31
  Pasta with Seafood Sauce, 32–33
  sauce, red, linguine with, 15–16

cooking, passion for, 1–5
cooking time. *See* time
cream cheese
    olive-caper spread, 255
        and salami sandwiches, 200
    Prosciutto, Pâté, and Camembert
        Sandwiches, 182
    Prosciutto, Shrimp, and Country
        Cream Sandwiches, 209
cream sauce, garlic, 237
cream sauce, turkey meatball sand-
    wiches with, 185–86
Creamed Tomato-Caper Sauce, 232
    tortellini with smoked salmon and,
        79
Crema all'Aglio, 237
Crema di Capperi e Olive, 244
Crema di Pomodoro e Capperi, 232
cucumber, in Shrimp Cake Sandwiches
    with Tartar Sauce, 206–7
curried shrimp and scallops, lasagnette
    with, 54–55
Curry Sauce, 236

dough, for pizza, 127
    Sicilian-style, 128
dumplings
    chicken, 224
    pizza, 141–44

Egg Buns, 174–75
eggplant
    fried, sandwiches, 189–90
    Pasta Boats, 26–27
    Pasta with Prosciutto-and-Vegetable
        Sauce, 19–20
    pizza with olives, capers, and,
        156–57
    roasted, pizza with sausage, pro-
        volone, and, 158–59
    sauce, baked pasta with, 11–12
    timbale of lasagna and, 77–78
eggs, hard-boiled
    Meatloaf Sandwiches, 194–95
    Stuffed Pizza San Vito, 166–67
    Timbale of Eggplant and Lasagna,
        77–78

*Fagottini di Pizza con Salame e Funghi di
    Bosco*, 146–47
fennel
    and prosciutto pizza, creamy, 137–38

risotto with pancetta, Parmesan, and,
    112–13
flatbread, garlic-rosemary, 145
Fontina, 106
    and asparagus sauce, 247–48
        pappardelle with, 69
    and prosciutto pizza, creamy, 137–38
    sandwiches, mushroom, truffle, and,
        191–92

garlic
    cream sauce, 237
        meat tortellini with, 58–59
    roasted
        fried pizza dumplings stuffed with
            spinach, ricotta, and, 143–44
        green pansoti with potatoes and, 49
        pizza with caramelized onion,
            prosciutto, Gorgonzola, and,
            154–55
        pulp, 251
        sauce, 251
        Timbale of Eggplant and Lasagna,
            77–78
        zucchini-filled half-moons, 51–52
    -rosemary flatbread, 145
    stewed, green lasagna with pine nuts,
        ricotta, and, 47–48
gnocchi, 4–5, 91–95
    with Arriminata Sauce, 103
    bread, with tomato sauce, 97–98
    with Orvieto Sauce, 102
    ricotta-and-spinach, 99–100
    with Turkey and Bell Pepper Sauce,
        101
goat cheese, pizza with sausage and, 160
Gorgonzola
    Four-Cheese Pizza, 131
    pasta with sauce of beets, sausage,
        and, 28–29
    pasta with sauce of spinach, pro-
        sciutto, and, 36–37
    pizza with caramelized onion,
        roasted garlic, prosciutto, and,
        154–55
    risotto with sausage, radicchio, and,
        116–17
Green Lasagna with Pine Nuts, Ri-
    cotta, and Stewed Garlic, 47–48
Green Pansoti with Potatoes and
    Roasted Garlic, 49
Gruyère, in Fried Calzones, 139–40

ham
    -and-cheese sandwiches, breaded,
        180–81
    Chicken Salad Sandwiches, 187–88
    See also prosciutto
Hamburgers Italiano, 193
herbs
    Chicken Stock, 223–24
    Fried Pizza Dumplings Stuffed with
        Meat Sauce, 141–42
    Garlic-Rosemary Flatbread, 145
    Pasta with Prosciutto-and-Vegetable
        Sauce, 19–20
    sage, risotto with pumpkin, sausage,
        and, 108–9
    Turkey and Bell Pepper Sauce, 241
    Vegetarian Lasagnette, 82–83
hors d'oeuvres
    asparagus cream, 199
    chicken, 184
    olive-caper cream cheese, 200,
        255
    See also panini; sandwiches

Impasto per la Pizza, 127
Impasto alla Siciliana, 128
Italian cooking, 2–4
Italian-Style Bread Crumbs, 220

lamb
    ground
        Hamburgers Italiano, 193
        Meat Sauce, 225
        meatball sandwiches with minted
            tomato sauce, 178
        Meatloaf Sandwiches, 194–95
        pappardelle with, 64
    sauce, rustic, 228
lasagna (*lasagne*)
    green, with pine nuts, ricotta, and
        stewed garlic, 47–48
    timbale of eggplant and, 77–78
    white (*in bianco*), 53
lasagnette
    with curried shrimp and scallops,
        54–55
    vegetarian, 82–83
leeks
    pasta medallions with ricotta, pro-
        sciutto, and, 60–61
    Pasta with Prosciutto-and-Vegetable
        Sauce, 19–20

leftovers
  chicken, from stock, 224
  gnocchi, to reheat, 95
  risotto cakes, 109
Ligurian Sauce, 238
  Potato Pizza, 165
  stuffed pasta with, 80–81
Linguine with Red Clam Sauce,
  15–16
Lobster Ravioli, 56–57
Lucca-style chickpea pizza, 136

mantecatura, 106
Mantua (Mantova)
  cannelloni in the style of, 45–46
  tomato sauce in the style of, 231
Margherita, pizza, 152
mascarpone
  Fontina, Mushroom, and Truffle
    Sandwiches, 191–92
  Olive-Caper Cream Cheese Spread,
    255
  Prosciutto and Asparagus Cream
    Sandwiches, 198–99
  prosciutto sandwiches with mint,
    Parmesan, and, 179
  Veal Cutlet Sandwiches, 210–11
Meat Sauce, 225
  fried pizza dumplings stuffed with,
    141–42
  white, 227
Meat Tortellini with Garlic Cream
  Sauce, 58–59
Meatloaf Sandwiches, 194–95
medallions, pasta (*medaglioni di pasta*)
  with leeks, ricotta, and prosciutto,
    60–61
  with wild mushrooms and truffle,
    62–63
Mezzelune al Gambero, 50
*Mezzelune di Zucchine con Sugo all'Aglio
  Arrostito*, 51–52
mint, prosciutto sandwiches with
  mascarpone, Parmesan, and,
  179
minted tomato sauce, lamb meatball
  sandwiches with, 178
mistakes, 1–2, 38
mortadella, 17, 18
  sauce, pasta with, 17–18
  Stuffed Pasta with Ligurian Sauce,
    80–81

mozzarella, 12
  Breaded Ham-and-Cheese Sand-
    wiches (*in carrozza*), 180–81
  calzones with prosciutto and, 130
  Cannelloni Mantua Style, 45–46
  Fried Eggplant Sandwiches, 189–90
  Fried Pizza Dumplings Stuffed with
    Meat Sauce, 141–42
  Pasta Boats, 26–27
  pasta with eggplant sauce, 11–12
  pasta with sausage and zucchini,
    13–14
pizza
  American-style pepperoni, 149
  braised-pepper, 134–35
  four-cheese, 131
  four seasons, 150–51
  Margherita, 152
  Neapolitan, 148
  with olives, capers, and eggplant,
    156–57
  with prosciutto and mushrooms,
    153
  with roasted eggplant, sausage, and
    provolone, 158–59
  with shrimp, scallops, and
    pancetta, 161–62
  with spinach, tomatoes, and pine
    nuts, 163–64
  stuffed, with prosciutto, arti-
    chokes, and three cheeses,
    168–69
  Timbale of Eggplant and Lasagna,
    77–78
mushrooms
  Orvieto Sauce, 243–44
  pasta with pancetta, clams, and,
    30–31
  Pizza Four Seasons, 150–51
  pizza with prosciutto and, 153
  pizza rounds stuffed with salami and,
    146–47
  portobello, and cheese sandwiches,
    196–97
  risotto with peas, pancetta, and,
    114–15
  sandwiches, Fontina, truffle, and,
    191–92
  wild, pasta medallions with truffle
    and, 62–63
mussels, in Pasta with Seafood Sauce,
  32–33

noodles, fresh, 64.
  See also pappardelle
nuts, toasting, 29, 48, 199

oil
  in cooking pasta, 7–8
  truffle, 63, 106
olives
  black
    Olive-Caper Cream Cheese
      Spread, 200, 255
    Pasta Boats, 26–27
    pizza with capers, eggplant, and,
      156–57
    Pizza Four Seasons, 150–51
  green, pimiento-stuffed
    Olive-Caper Cream Cheese
      Spread, 255
    Sandwiches Tartare, 201
    Tuna Salad Sandwiches, 208
onions
  caramelized, pizza with roasted
    garlic, prosciutto, Gorgonzola,
    and, 154–55
  sandwiches, sausage, pepper, and,
    202–3
  Vegetarian Lasagnette, 82–83
Orlando, Leoluca, 214–16
Orvieto Sauce, 243–44
  gnocchi with, 102

Palermo-style pizza, 129
palm hearts, in Chicken Salad Sandwiches, 187–88
pancetta
  Baked Pasta with Sausage and Zuc-
    chini, 13–14
  Orvieto Sauce, 243–44
  pasta with clams, mushrooms, and,
    30–31
  pizza with shrimp, scallops, and,
    161–62
  risotto with fennel, Parmesan, and,
    112–13
  risotto with peas, mushrooms, and,
    114–15
  Ustica Sauce, 252
Pane e Panelle, 212–13
panini, 5, 173
  all'uovo (Egg Buns), 174–75
  See also sandwiches
Pansoti con Salsa Ligure, 80–81

Pansoti Verdi con Patate e Aglio Arrostito, 49

pappardelle
  with artichokes, prosciutto, and truffle, 65–66
  with Fontina and Asparagus Sauce, 69
  with Rustic Lamb Sauce, 64

Parma Sauce, 240

Pumpkin Ravioli, 70–71

Parmesan, 106
  American-Style Pepperoni Pizza, 149
  Artichoke Ravioli, 42–44
  béchamel sauce, 235
    Vegetarian Lasagnette, 82–83
  Caesar Sandwich Spread, 253
  Cannelloni Mantua Style, 45–46
  Chicken Caesar Sandwiches, 183–84
  Chickpea Pizza Lucca Style, 136
  Creamy Fennel and Prosciutto Pizza, 137–38
  Fontina and Asparagus Sauce, 247–48
  Four-Cheese Pizza, 131
  Fried Eggplant Sandwiches, 189–90
  Fried Pizza Dumplings Stuffed with Spinach, Ricotta, and Roasted Garlic, 143–44
  Garlic-Rosemary Flatbread, 145
  gnocchi, 94–95
    with Orvieto Sauce, 102
    with Turkey and Bell Pepper Sauce, 101
  Green Lasagna with Pine Nuts, Ricotta, and Stewed Garlic, 47–48
  Green Pansoti with Potatoes and Roasted Garlic, 49
  Ligurian Sauce, 238
  Meat Tortellini with Garlic Cream Sauce, 58–59
  Pappardelle with Artichokes, Prosciutto, and Truffle, 65–66

pasta
  medallions with leeks, ricotta, and prosciutto, 60–61
  medallions with wild mushrooms and truffle, 62–63
  with mortadella sauce, 17–18
  with prosciutto-and-vegetable sauce, 19–20
  with ricotta-and-saffron sauce, 21–22

Pizza with Prosciutto and Mushrooms, 153

Prosciutto and Asparagus Cream Sandwiches, 198–99

prosciutto sandwiches with mint, mascarpone, and, 179

Prosciutto, Shrimp, and Country Cream Sandwiches, 209

Pumpkin Ravioli, 70–71

Ravioli with Calabrian Sauce with Sausage, 67–68

Ricotta and Spinach Gnocchi, 99–100

risotto
  with fennel, pancetta, and, 112–13
  with peas, pancetta, and mushrooms, 114–15
  with pumpkin, sausage, and sage, 108–9
  with sausage, radicchio, and Gorgonzola, 116–17

Sausage and Provolone Sandwiches with Tomato Sauce, 204–5

Sicilian Street Sandwiches, 212–13

Stuffed Pasta with Ligurian Sauce, 80–81

Stuffed Pizza with Prosciutto, Artichokes, and Three Cheeses, 168–69

Tagliatelle with Piedmontese Sauce, 76

Tuna Salad Sandwiches, 208

Turkey Meatball Sandwiches with Cream Sauce, 185–86

Veal Cutlet Sandwiches, 210–11

Vegetarian Lasagnette, 82–83

White Lasagna, 53

Zucchini-Filled Half-Moons with Roasted Garlic Sauce, 51–52

pasta, 4, 7–9
  baked, with Eggplant Sauce, 11–12
  baked, with sausage and zucchini, 13–14
  with beet, sausage, and Gorgonzola sauce, 28–29
  boats (*Barchette di Pasta*), 26–27
  Cannelloni Mantua Style, 45–46
  fresh (*pasta fresca*), 10, 38–41
    Artichoke Ravioli, 42–44
    Lasagnette with Curried Shrimp and Scallops, 54–55
    Lobster Ravioli, 56–57

Meat Tortellini with Garlic Cream Sauce, 58–59

medallions with leeks, ricotta, and prosciutto, 60–61

medallions with wild mushrooms and truffle, 62–63

Pappardelle with Artichokes, Prosciutto, and Truffle, 65–66

Pappardelle with Fontina and Asparagus Sauce, 69

Pappardelle with Rustic Lamb Sauce, 64

Pumpkin Ravioli, 70–71

Ravioli with Calabrian Sauce with Sausage, 67–68

Sausage Ravioli, 72–73

Scallop Tortellini with Pea Sauce and Prosciutto, 74–75

Shrimp-Filled Half-Moons, 50

spinach, 41

Stuffed Pasta with Ligurian Sauce, 80–81

Tortellini with Smoked Salmon and Creamed Tomato-Caper Sauce, 79

Zucchini-Filled Half-Moons with Roasted Garlic Sauce, 51–52

Green Lasagna with Pine Nuts, Ricotta, and Stewed Garlic, 47–48

Green Pansoti with Potatoes and Roasted Garlic, 49

Lasagnette with Curried Shrimp and Scallops, 54–55

Linguine with Red Clam Sauce, 15–16

with mortadella sauce, 17–18

with pancetta, clams, and mushrooms, 30–31

Pappardelle with Artichokes, Prosciutto, and Truffle, 65–66

Pappardelle with Fontina and Asparagus Sauce, 69

Pappardelle with Rustic Lamb Sauce, 64

with pecorino and salami, 25

with prosciutto-and-vegetable sauce, 19–20

with ricotta-and-saffron sauce, 21–22

Scallop Tortellini with Pea Sauce and Prosciutto, 74–75

with seafood sauce, 32–33

Shrimp-Filled Half-Moons, 50

pasta (*cont.*)
    with shrimp sauce, 34–35
    with spinach, Gorgonzola, and pro-
        sciutto sauce, 36–37
    stuffed, with Ligurian Sauce, 80–81
    swordfish picchio pacchio, 23–24
    Tagliatelle with Piedmontese Sauce,
        76
    Timbale of Eggplant and Lasagna,
        77–78
    Tortellini with Smoked Salmon and
        Creamed Tomato-Caper Sauce,
        79
    Vegetarian Lasagnette, 82–83
    White Lasagna, 53
    Zucchini-Filled Half-Moons with
        Roasted Garlic Sauce, 51–52
pâté, sandwiches, prosciutto, Camem-
    bert, and, 182
peas
    Fried Pizza Dumplings Stuffed with
        Meat Sauce, 141–42
    Pasta with Prosciutto-and-Vegetable
        Sauce, 19–20
    risotto with pancetta, mushrooms
        and, 114–15
    sauce, 249
        scallop tortellini with prosciutto
            and, 74–75
    Stuffed Pizza with Prosciutto, Arti-
        chokes, and Three Cheeses,
        168–69
pecorino, pasta with salami and, 25
Peperonata al Tacchino, 241
pepperoni
    American-Style pizza, 149
    Hamburgers Italiano, 193
peppers, bell, 203
    Braised-Pepper Pizza, 134–35
    Chicken Caesar Sandwiches, 184
    pasta with prosciutto-and-
        vegetable sauce, 19–20
    sandwiches, sausage, onion, and,
        202–3
    Turkey Meatball Sandwiches with
        Cream Sauce, 185–86
    and turkey sauce, 241
        gnocchi and, 101
pesto, in Portobello Mushroom and
    Cheese Sandwiches, 196–97
picchipacchio, 23
Piedmontese Sauce, 239
    tagliatelle with, 76

pine nuts (*pinoli*)
    Fried Eggplant Sandwiches, 189–90
    green lasagna with ricotta, stewed
        garlic, and, 47–48
    Ligurian Sauce, 238
        stuffed pasta with, 80–81
    pizza with spinach, tomatoes, and,
        163–64
    Prosciutto and Asparagus Cream
        Sandwiches, 198–99
    toasting, 48, 199
pizza, 5, 125–26
    agliata al rosmarino, 145
    American-style pepperoni, 149
    braised-pepper, 134–35
    with caramelized onion, roasted gar-
        lic, prosciutto, and Gorgonzola,
        154–55
    chickpea, Lucca style, 136
    dough for, 127
        Sicilian-style, 128
    dumplings, fried
        stuffed with meat sauce, 141–42
        stuffed with spinach, ricotta, and
            roasted garlic, 143–44
    fennel and prosciutto, creamy,
        137–38
    four-cheese, 131
    four seasons (*quattro stagioni*), 150–51
    Margherita, 152
    Neapolitan (*napoletana*), 148
    with olives, capers, and eggplant
        (*caponata*), 156–57
    Palermo style (*sfincionello*), 129
    potato, 165
    with prosciutto and mushrooms, 153
    with roasted eggplant, sausage, and
        provolone, 158–59
    rolls, with sausage and ricotta,
        132–33
    rounds, stuffed with salami and
        mushrooms, 146–47
    with sausage and goat cheese, 160
    with shrimp, scallops, and pancetta
        (*mare e monti*), 161–62
    with spinach, tomatoes, and pine
        nuts, 163–64
    stuffed, 5, 169
        with prosciutto, artichokes, and
            three cheeses, 168–69
        with radicchio, prosciutto, and
            Camembert, 170–71
    San Vito, 166–67

pork, in Meatloaf Sandwiches, 194–95
potatoes
    green pansoti with roasted garlic
        and, 49
    pizza, 165
    Sicilian Street Sandwiches, 212–13
prosciutto
    calzones with mozzarella and, 130
    Cannelloni Mantua Style, 45–46
    and fennel pizza, creamy, 137–38
    Fried Calzones, 139–40
    Meat Sauce, 225
        fried pizza dumplings stuffed with,
            141–42
    Meat Tortellini with Garlic Cream
        Sauce, 58–59
    pappardelle with artichokes, truffle,
        and, 65–66
    Parma Sauce, 240
    pasta medallions with leeks, ricotta,
        and, 60–61
    pasta with sauce of spinach, Gor-
        gonzola, and, 36–37
    Piedmontese Sauce, 239
    pizza
        with caramelized onion, roasted
            garlic, Gorgonzola, and, 154–55
        four seasons, 150–51
        with mushrooms and, 153
        stuffed, with artichokes, three
            cheeses, and, 168–69
        stuffed, with radicchio, Camem-
            bert, and, 170–71
    sandwiches
        asparagus cream and, 198–99
        breaded ham-and-cheese (*Mozza-
            rella in Carrozza*), 180–81
        with mint, mascarpone, Parmesan,
            and, 179
        pâté, Camembert, and, 182
        shrimp, country cream, and, 209
        scallop tortellini with pea sauce
            and, 74–75
        and vegetable sauce, 19–20
    White Meat Sauce, 227
provolone
    Braised-Pepper Pizza, 134–35
    Hamburgers Italiano, 193
    Lamb Meatball Sandwiches with
        Minted Tomato Sauce, 178
    Meatloaf Sandwiches, 194–95
    pizza
        potato, 165

provolone, on pizza (*cont.*)
    with prosciutto and mushrooms, 153
    with roasted eggplant, sausage, and, 158–59
    with sausage and goat cheese, 160
    stuffed, with prosciutto, artichokes, and three cheeses, 168–69
    sandwiches, sausage and, with Tomato Sauce, 204–5
pumpkin
    ravioli, 70–71
    risotto with sausage, sage, and, 10

Quick Shrimp Sauce, 250

radicchio
    risotto with sausage, Gorgonzola, and, 116–17
    stuffed pizza with prosciutto, Camembert, and, 170–71
Ragù di Agnello alla Rustica, 228
Ragù in Bianco, 227
Ragù di Carne, 225
Ravazzate Fritte al Sugo di Carne, 141–42
Ravazzate di Magro con Aglio Arrostito, 143–44
ravioli
    artichoke, 42–44
    with Calabrian Sauce with Sausage, 67–68
    lobster, 56–57
    pumpkin, 70–71
    sausage, 72–73
red clam sauce, linguine with, 15–16
rice, varieties for risotto, 105.
    See also risotto
ricotta
    Cannelloni Mantua Style, 45–46
    fried pizza dumplings stuffed with spinach, roasted garlic, and, 143–44
    green lasagna with pine nuts, stewed garlic, and, 47–48
    pasta with Ligurian Sauce, 80–81
    pasta medallions with leeks, prosciutto, and, 60–61
    pizza rolls with sausage and, 132–33
    -and-saffron sauce, for pasta, 21–22
    Sausage Ravioli, 72–73

-and-spinach gnocchi, 99–100
Stuffed Pizza Rounds with Salami and Mushrooms, 146–47
Stuffed Pizza San Vito, 166–67
Veal Cutlet Sandwiches, 210–11
Zucchini-Filled Half-Moons with Roasted Garlic Sauce, 51–52
risotto, 105–7
    black squid, 110–11
    with fennel, pancetta, and Parmesan, 112–13
    with peas, pancetta, and mushrooms, 114–15
    with pumpkin, sausage, and sage, 108–9
    with sausage, radicchio, and Gorgonzola, 116–17
rock shrimp, 35
Rollini al Forno con Salsiccia e Ricotta, 132–33
rolls. *See* Egg Buns; *panini;* pizza rolls; sandwiches; Sicilian Buns
Romano
    Baked Pasta with Sausage and Zucchini, 13–14
    Baked Pizza Rolls with Sausage and Ricotta, 132–33
    Bread Gnocchi with Tomato Sauce, 97–98
    Chicken Caesar Sandwiches, 183–84
    Fried Eggplant Sandwiches, 189–90
    Fried Pizza Dumplings Stuffed with Spinach, Ricotta, and Roasted Garlic, 143–44
    Gnocchi with Arriminata Sauce, 103
    Hamburgers Italiano, 193
    Lamb Meatball Sandwiches with Minted Tomato Sauce, 178
    Meatloaf Sandwiches, 194–95
    Pasta Boats, 26–27
    Pasta with Pecorino and Salami, 25
    Pizza with Olives, Capers, and Eggplant, 156–57
    Pizza Palermo Style, 129
    Ravioli with Calabrian Sauce with Sausage, 67–68
    Sausage Ravioli, 72–73
    Shrimp Cake Sandwiches with Tartar Sauce, 206–7
    Stuffed Pizza Rounds with Salami and Mushrooms, 146–47
    Stuffed Pizza San Vito, 166–67

Turkey Meatball Sandwiches with Cream Sauce, 185–86
Veal Cutlet Sandwiches, 210–11
rosemary-garlic flatbread, 145
rules in cooking, 2–4
Rustic Lamb Sauce, 228
    pappardelle with, 64

saffron, 21
    -and-ricotta sauce, for pasta, 21–22
sage, risotto with pumpkin, sausage, and, 108–9
salami
    Green Pansoti with Potatoes and Roasted Garlic, 49
    Pasta Boats, 26–27
    pasta with pecorino and, 25
    Pasta with Ricotta-and-Saffron Sauce, 21–22
    Piedmontese Sauce, 239
    pizza rounds stuffed with mushrooms and, 146–47
    sandwiches, olive-caper cream cheese and, 200
    Stuffed Pizza San Vito, 166–67
salmon, smoked, tortellini with Creamed Tomato-Caper Sauce and, 79
Salsa Arriminata, 245–46
Salsa al Curry, 236
Salsa Ligure, 238
Salsa Tartara, 254
San Vito, stuffed pizza, 166–67
sandwiches (*panini*)
    Caesar spread for, 253
    chicken Caesar, 183–84
    chicken salad, 187–88
    Fontina, mushroom, and truffle, 191–92
    fried eggplant, 189–90
    ham-and-cheese, breaded (*Mozzarella in Carrozza*), 180–81
    Hamburgers Italiano, 193
    lamb meatball, with minted tomato sauce, 178
    meatloaf, 194–95
    olive-caper cream cheese spread, 255
    portobello mushroom and cheese, 196–97
    prosciutto
        and asparagus cream, 198–99
        pâté, Camembert, and, 182

sandwiches (*cont.*)
    shrimp, country cream, and (*mare e monti*), 209
    with mint, mascarpone, and Parmesan, 179
    salami and olive-caper cream cheese, 200
    sausage, pepper, and onion, 202–3
    sausage and provolone, with Tomato Sauce, 204–5
    shrimp cake, with tartar sauce, 206–7
    Sicilian street, 212–13
    tartare, 201
    tuna salad, 208
    turkey meatball, with cream sauce, 185–86
    veal cutlet, 210–11
    See also panini
sauce (*salsa; sugo*)
    arriminata, 245–46
    béchamel, 234–35
    Calabrian, with sausage, 242
    creamed tomato-caper, 79, 232
    curry, 236
    Fontina and asparagus, 247–48
    garlic, roasted, 251
    garlic cream, 237
    lamb, rustic, 228
    Ligurian, 238
    meat, 225
    meat, white, 227
    Orvieto, 243–44
    Parma, 240
    parmesan béchamel, 235
    pea, 249
    Piedmontese, 239
    pizza, 233
    shrimp, quick, 250
    tartar, 254
    tomato, 229
        Mantua style, 231
        spicy, 230
    turkey and bell pepper, 241
    Ustica, 252
saucing of pasta, 8
sausage, Italian-style
    pasta with eggplant sauce, 11–12
    pasta with sauce of beets, Gorgonzola, and, 28–29
    Piedmontese Sauce, 239
    pizza with roasted eggplant, provolone, and, 158–59

spicy
    Hamburgers Italiano, 193
    pasta with zucchini and, 13–14
    pizza with goat cheese and, 160
    pizza rolls with ricotta and, 132–33
    ravioli, 72–73
    sandwiches, provolone and, with Tomato Sauce, 204–5
    Stuffed Pizza San Vito, 166–67
sweet
    Arriminata Sauce, 245–46
    Calabrian sauce with, 67–68, 242
    risotto with pumpkin, sage, and, 108–9
    risotto with radicchio, Gorgonzola, and, 116–17
    sandwiches, pepper, onion, and, 202–3
scallops
    lasagnette with curried shrimp and, 54–55
    Pasta with Seafood Sauce, 32–33
    pizza with shrimp, pancetta, and, 161–62
    tortellini with pea sauce and prosciutto, 74–75
seafood
    Black Squid Risotto, 110–11
    Lasagnette with Curried Shrimp and Scallops, 54–55
    Linguine with Red Clam Sauce, 15–16
    Lobster Ravioli, 56–57
    Pasta with Seafood Sauce, 32–33
    Pasta with Shrimp Sauce, 34–35
    Pizza with Shrimp, Scallops, and Pancetta, 161–62
    Prosciutto, Shrimp, and Country Cream Sandwiches, 209
    Quick Shrimp Sauce, 250
    Scallop Tortellini with Pea Sauce and Prosciutto, 74–75
    Shrimp Cake Sandwiches with Tartar Sauce, 206–7
    Shrimp-Filled Half-Moons, 50
    Swordfish Picchio Pacchio Pasta, 23–24
    Tuna Salad Sandwiches, 208
Sfincione di San Vito, 166–67

Sfincionelli, 129, 176–77
shrimp, 35
    half-moons filled with, 50
    lasagnette with curried scallops and, 54–55
    Pasta with Seafood Sauce, 32–33
    pizza with scallops, pancetta, and, 161–62
    sandwiches
        prosciutto, country cream, and, 209
        shrimp cake, with tartar sauce, 206–7
    sauce, quick, 250
        pasta with, 34–35
Sicilian Buns, 176–77
Sicilian Street Sandwiches, 212–13
Sicilian-style pizza, 125
    dough for, 128
snacks; 173. *See also* hors d'oeuvres; leftovers; *panini;* pizza; sandwiches
soppressata
    Meatloaf Sandwiches, 194–95
    Pasta with Ricotta-and-Saffron Sauce, 21–22
spinach
    fresh pasta sheets, 41
        Green Lasagna with Pine Nuts, Ricotta, and Stewed Garlic, 47–48
        Green Pansoti with Potatoes and Roasted Garlic, 49
    Ligurian Sauce, 238
    pasta with sauce of Gorgonzola, prosciutto, and, 36–37
    pizza dumplings stuffed with ricotta, roasted garlic, and, 143–44
    pizza with tomatoes, pine nuts, and, 163–64
    Stuffed Pizza San Vito, 166–67
    -and-ricotta gnocchi, 99–100
squid risotto, black, 110–11
stock, 219
    beef, 221–22
    chicken, 223–24
Swordfish Picchio Pacchio Pasta, 23–24

Tagliatelle with Piedmontese Sauce, 76
Tartar Sauce, 254
    shrimp cake sandwiches with, 206–7
Timbale of Eggplant and Lasagna, 77–78